Evidence, Answers, & Christian Faith

Evidence, Answers, & Christian Faith

PROBING THE HEADLINES
THAT IMPACT YOUR FAMILY

Jimmy Williams

General Editor

Kregel
Publications

Evidence, Answers, & Christian Faith: Probing the Headlines That Impact Your Family

© 2002 by Probe Ministries

Published by Kregel Publications, a division of Kregel, Inc., P.O. Box 2607, Grand Rapids, MI 49501. Kregel Publications provides trusted, biblical publications for Christian growth and service. Your comments and suggestions are valued.

Unless otherwise indicated, Scripture quotations are from the *New American Standard Bible,* © the Lockman Foundation 1960, 1962, 1963, 1968, 1971, 1972, 1973, 1975, 1977.

Scripture marked NIV taken from the *Holy Bible: New International Version®.* © 1973, 1978, 1984 by International Bible Society. Used by permission of Zondervan Publishing House. All rights reserved.

Scripture quotations marked KJV are from the King James version of the Holy Bible.

For more information about Kregel Publications, visit our Web site: www.kregel.com.

Library of Congress Cataloging-in-Publication Data
Evidence, answers, and Christian faith: probing the headlines that impact your famliy / James F. Williams, general editor.
  p. cm.
Includes bibliographical references.
  1. Apologetics. I. Williams, James F.
BT1103 .E85   2002   239—dc 21   2002005522

ISBN 0-8254-2035-0

Printed in the United States of America

02 03 04 05 06 / 5 4 3 2 1

Contents

Foreword

The Christian faith is based on evidence. God has revealed Himself to us through His written Word, through His crucified and resurrected Son, and by the witness of the Holy Spirit. In addition to multiple, credible witnesses to the events of the Scriptures, Christianity is founded on demonstrable, indisputable facts. We are incredibly privileged to have this revelation; without it, we could not experience fellowship with God or gain eternal life with Him. Presenting this evidence—this defense—of the truth of Christianity is the purview of *apologetics.*

The apostle Peter wrote, "Always be prepared to give an answer to everyone who asks you to give the reason for the hope that you have" (1 Peter 3:15 NIV). But today, as Rick Wade points out in his introduction, "[Apologetics] includes more than a defense . . . a second task of apologetics is to challenge other people to defend *their* beliefs."

Apologetics is, however, more than intellectual sparring over theology. We must be prepared, asserts Wade, to respond to "the challenges of our day"—what Jimmy Williams, in his chapter "Apologetics and Evangelism," refers to as "develop[ing] a complete apologetic," that is, addressing "one's ethics, one's emotional connection, and one's logical presentation." To be credible carriers of the message, Christians must appeal to the whole person. I have known Jimmy Williams for over thirty years, and he has consistently modeled this "complete apologetic" in his personal walk with God and through his effective ministry.

In essence, apologetics rests on this: Jesus either was or was not who He said He was; the Bible is either true or untrue. There is no middle ground. If Jesus was not God in the flesh, then He was a liar and, thus, not even a good man. Each person must examine the evidence and reach a verdict.

I trust that God will use this book to reveal Himself to those who are earnestly seeking the truth.

—STEPHEN B. DOUGLASS
President, Campus Crusade for Christ

Contributors

Don Closson is the director of administration for Probe Ministries as well as a vital part of Probe's research team. He holds a B.S. degree in education from Southern Illinois University, an M.S. degree in educational administration from Illinois State University, and an M.S. degree *(cum laude)* in biblical studies from Dallas Theological Seminary. Before joining Probe Ministries in 1986, as a research associate in the field of education, Don served as a public school teacher and administrator.

Rick Rood is the former director of publications at Probe Ministries and now serves as a hospital chaplain. A graduate of Seattle Pacific University (B.A., history) and Dallas Theological Seminary (Th.M), Rick also has completed coursework (A.B.D.) for his Ph.D. degree in theology at Dallas Seminary. He has served as a pastor and a seminary instructor and ministered with an international students' organization for seven years. Rick and his wife, Polly, are the parents of two young adults.

Rick Wade is a research associate for Probe Ministries. He holds a B.A. degree in communications (radio broadcasting) from Moody Bible Institute and an M.A. degree *(cum laude)* in Christian thought (theology/philosophy of religion) from Trinity Evangelical Divinity School, where his studies culminated in a thesis on the apologetics of Carl F. H. Henry.

Jimmy Williams is the founder (1973) and former president of Probe Ministries. He is currently serving with Probe as minister-at-large. Jimmy has been involved in university ministry for forty years, visiting 181 campuses in the United States, Canada, Central America, Europe, and Russia. Holding a B.A. degree from Southern Methodist University and a Th.M. degree from Dallas Theological Seminary, Jimmy has also completed coursework in interdisciplinary doctoral studies (A.B.D.) at the University of Texas-Dallas. Before he founded Probe, he served with Campus Crusade for Christ from 1961 to 1973.

Pat Zukeran is a research associate as well as a national and international speaker for Probe Ministries. He graduated from Point Loma Nazarene University in San Diego, California, and holds a Th.M. degree from Dallas Theological Seminary. Before joining the staff of Probe Ministries, Pat served in the pastorate for ten years. He is the author of the book *Unless I See . . . Reasons to Consider the Christian Faith.*

Part 1

Foundational Issues

1

Christian Apologetics

An Introduction

Rick Wade

Throughout the history of the church, Christians have been called upon to explain why we believe what we believe. The apostle Paul spoke of his ministry as "the defense and confirmation of the gospel" (Phil. 1:7), and Peter said to be "ready to make a defense to everyone who asks you" (1 Peter 3:15). Such activity came to be known by the church as apologetics, which means "defense." If it is important that we defend the faith, how do we do it?

This chapter, rather than providing evidence and arguments, looks at basic principles for guiding Christians in defending the faith. This chapter examines first the importance of thinking logically and looks at the specific charge, so prevalent on college campuses today, of Christian *elitism*. It then presents a valid case for Christianity.

The chief concern of apologetics relates to the truth of Jesus Christ. In the days of the Greeks, when someone was summoned to court to face a charge, that person would present an *apology,* or a *defense.* For Christians, such a defense might mean answering the question, "Why do you believe that Jesus is God?" or it might mean answering a question more often heard today: "Why do you think that Christians have *the* truth?"

So although apologetics is, first, a defense, it includes more than a defense. At issue is the truth of not only our beliefs but also the beliefs of others. So a second task of apologetics is to challenge other people to defend *their* beliefs.

A third task of apologetics is to present a case for the truth of the biblical message. One might call this task "proving" Christianity. But if this goal seems to be too ambitious, we might speak simply of persuading people of the truth of the biblical message.

In all of this, the goal is to let the light of God's truth shine in all its brilliance. It is a worthy ambition, also, to bring nonbelievers to a recognition of the truth of Jesus Christ and to persuade them to put their faith in Him.

Apologetics is typically a response to a specific question or challenge that is either stated explicitly or merely implied. Paul reasoned with the Jews, for whom the Cross was a stumbling block, "explaining and giving evidence that the Christ had to suffer and rise again from the dead" (Acts 17:3). But in the second century, apologists defended not only Christian beliefs but also Christians themselves against such charges as atheism, cannibalism, and being threats to the state. In the Medieval era, apologetists devoted more attention to the challenges presented by Judaism and Islam. In the era of the Enlightenment, apologists defended Christianity against the narrow confines of scientific rationalism. Today, the challenge has shifted again, this time from attacks on specific doctrines to the question of whether Christianity has any claim at all to absolute truth.

Like our forebears, we must answer the challenges of our day. We must respond to our contemporaries' questions, as Peter admonishes us, regardless of how difficult and uncomfortable that might be.

Thinking Well

One of the frustrations in apologetics is addressing the myriad questions and challenges on one hand and presenting the supporting evidences and reasons on the other hand. Although it behooves us to master a certain level of both answering questions and presenting evidence, it is just as important to learn how to think well.

Thinking well, or logically, is important for Christians for several reasons. It helps us put together the various pieces of our faith to form a cohesive whole. It helps us make decisions in everyday life. Even when the Bible doesn't speak directly to a particular issue, we can draw true beliefs or proper courses of action from what Scripture *does* tell us.

Logical thinking is especially important for an apologist. On one hand, it prevents us from presenting shoddy arguments for what we believe. On the other hand, it helps us evaluate the beliefs of those who challenge Christianity. Too often, we stumble at criticisms that sound good but that, in reality, stand on legs that are shaky in logic.

How, for example, does a Christian respond to someone who states, "There is no absolute truth"? If the individual speaking really thinks that no absolute truth—that is, truth that stands for all people at all times—exists, he or she can, at best, say only, "*In my opinion,* there is no absolute truth." Saying "There is no absolute truth" is stating an absolute; therefore, the statement refutes itself.

Another fallacious argument against the truth of Christianity is "All religions really teach the same thing." Christianity, however, does *not* teach the same thing as other religions. Christianity teaches that Jesus is God in the flesh;

other religions say, however, that He isn't. The principle of logic called the *law of noncontradiction* argues that Jesus can't both *be* God and *not be* God. Therefore, all religions clearly do not teach the same thing.

A third illogical argument against Christianity is, "I can't believe in Christ. Look at all the terrible things Christians have done through the centuries." Although the behavior of Christians does influence a non-Christian's responses to the gospel, such behavior has nothing to do with the truth of Christianity itself. If the gospel message proclaimed that once a person becomes a Christian that person will never sin again, then the objector would have grounds for questioning the truth of the faith. But the Bible makes no such claim. We can agree that Christians shouldn't do terrible things, but what Christians did in fourteenth-century Europe or what they do in twenty-first-century America in the name of Jesus doesn't change the reality of the incarnation, crucifixion, and resurrection of Christ. A nonbeliever might not like what people have done in the name of Jesus, but this complaint has no logical force against the truth of Christ.

Christians must discern if arguments against the faith are true and logically sound. Often, objections to Christianity are neither true nor logical. Learning how to think logically enables us to spot fallacies in the thinking of others. Pointing out these fallacies (gently, if possible) might cause the skeptic to rethink his or her position. At least it will defuse the attack on our faith.

Answering the Charge of Elitism

Logical thinking in apologetics applies to a charge being leveled against Christians today, especially on college campuses.

In a video, a young woman said that the notion that Christians have the only truth is elitist. With so many different beliefs in the world, the young woman asserted, how can any one group claim to have the only truth? Such thinking, she said, is arrogant.

How can Christians respond to this charge? First, note the name calling. Christians are charged with *elitism*, a word that, in a culture devoted to diversity, carries a negative connotation. By placing Christians in a defensive position, antagonists subordinate the real issue—a tactic that our culture often uses to attack ideas and positions. It is important, however, not to react in kind. Too often today, the battles over issues and ideas are fought with name calling and sloganeering, practices unbecoming to Christians and unprofitable in apologetics and evangelism. We must focus upon and deal with the ideas themselves.

Second, Christians can acknowledge that non-Christians can know truth and that other religions can include some truth. If a religion held no truth, it would find very few adherents. Other religions fail, though, on such fundamental issues as the identity of Jesus and the way to be reconciled to God.

Third, notice the faulty logic in the argument "There are many religions, and they are all equally valid." What does the mere existence of many points of view have to do with the truth-value of any of them? One might as easily say, "Some husbands think they should treat their wives with the same respect they themselves desire; some ignore their wives; other husbands think it's acceptable to beat their wives. Thus, one kind of treatment has as much merit as another." The structure of the argument is the same as that which states, "All religions are equally valid," but the conclusion obviously is wrong. A critic might understandably question our *assurance* that what we believe is *the* truth, given that so many people disagree. But it is faulty logic to conclude that *no* beliefs can claim final truth simply because so many of them exist.

Fourth, the argument against elitism rests upon the premise that two or more conflicting beliefs can be true. Such an assumption can be disproved by looking to everyday experience. My wife says that it is raining outside, but my son says that it isn't. It can't be both raining and not raining at the same time. Likewise, if one person says that Jesus is the only way to salvation and another person says that He isn't, only one person can be correct.

Some people will, of course, challenge the notion that our knowledge of God can be likened to our knowledge of rain. God is "wholly other," they say; we can't know Him through the things of this world. The issue of the depth to which we can know God is too involved to develop here and will be explored more fully in chapter 2. But thinking that we cannot know the nature of God seems to be a fundamental prejudice against authoritative revelation. God *has* spoken, and He has given us evidence in this world to confirm what He has said.

The preceding challenges to Christianity—and many others—are not easy to address. But if defending the faith means responding to the challenges of our day, we must prepare ourselves to do so, regardless of difficulty. Otherwise, we cannot expect to be heard.

The Case for Christianity—Foundational Considerations

Earlier, we noted that one task of apologetics is to present a case for the truth of the biblical message. Doing so involves some foundational issues, and we should examine them in considering the construction of a convincing case for Christianity.

When Christians are called upon to present a case for their faith, they are, in effect, being asked to offer proof that Christianity is true. What evidences or arguments can be marshaled to set forth and establish the truth of what we believe?

To make a case that no person of reasonable intelligence can fail to accept would be ideal. But the Bible acknowledges that many people will not believe no matter how compelling the evidence. Consider, for example, the story in Luke 16 about the rich man who died and suffered torment. He begged Abraham to send Lazarus back from the dead to warn his brothers about what they also faced. Abraham said, "If they do not listen to Moses and the Prophets, neither will they be persuaded if someone rises from the dead" (v. 31). A determined will can ignore the best of evidence.

Except for proofs in the mathematical sense, any proof is relative to each person; what will convince one person might not convince another. This fact doesn't mean, however, that Christianity becomes true only when someone is convinced; it is true regardless of whether anyone believes it.

In making a case for the faith, we seek to present a sound argument that will be persuasive for a particular listener. This consideration both frees us from the responsibility of presenting arguments that will convince everyone and does not burden us to depend upon a universal argument.

Even if we're able adequately to answer the challenges of a given individual, we must also be mindful of the real basis of our belief. A true knowledge of God is based upon divine testimony that is not only accepted by faith but also confirmed by evidence. The testimony of Scripture about such matters as the work of Christ on the cross and justification by faith cannot be proved; they can only be accepted by faith. Formidable and convincing reasons can be presented, however, for accepting this testimony as valid.

We must also bear in mind the nature of our message. Christianity is not just a system of beliefs but rather the message of the One who is truth. The claim of truth is especially pertinent today, given the mentality of modern culture. We seemingly have abandoned reasoning through the major issues of life in a disinterested, scientific manner and thereby coming to firm conclusions. Concepts that don't touch people where they live and how they feel hold little interest; therefore, we must draw people to Jesus as the answer to the major questions of life. Christianity is *living* truth, and it should be preached and defended as such.

If a nonbeliever becomes convinced that Christianity is at least plausible or believable, that's a good start. Often, it takes many steps for a skeptic to come to faith. Our task is to provide a solid intellectual foundation to help make those steps sure.

Presenting the Case for Christianity

The following outline offers a way to present a case for Christianity. It is up to you, the reader, to fill in the details through your own study.

Because God created the universe and is active in His creation, there is no lack of evidence for the truth of Christianity. The word *evidence* includes not only facts but also logical arguments and human experience. Evidence is anything that can be brought to bear on the truth-claims of Scripture.

In presenting evidence, be aware that the false

presuppositions that nonbelievers hold about God, man, and the world might skew their evaluation of the evidence. Also, the idea of encouraging people to evaluate Christianity makes even some Christians uneasy. Are we allowing sinful people to bring God to the bar of judgment? On the contrary, we are simply recognizing that, although the Bible never hints that anyone is ever justified in rejecting its message, Scripture presents its witness to the truth primarily through historical reminders and miracles. By offering supporting evidence *to* the Bible, we can appeal to nonbelievers based upon the remnants of their true understanding of the world—an understanding that they possess because they have been made in God's image and because they live in God's world.

The supporting evidence at our disposal can be divided into three categories: fact, or empirical evidence; reason, or logical thinking; and experience, or human nature, and the experience of life. These three kinds of evidence can be used in two ways: for evaluation and for explanation.

In presenting evidence that evaluates, we can first look for evidence in a given area that confirms Scripture. We can ask, for example, "Do observable facts affirm what Scripture teaches?" Consider, too, history and archeology. Are the teachings of Scripture coherent and logically consistent? Typically, people who talk about contradictions in the Bible have a hard time remembering one. Is what the Bible says about human nature and human experience true to what we know? Certainly we can identify with biblical characters.

In presenting evidence that explains, an apologist might ask the following questions. Does the Christian worldview explain the facts of nature? (It does because the Bible says that Jesus created and sustains the universe.) Does Christianity provide an explanation for the reliability of human reason itself? (It does because the Bible says that we are created with intelligence in the image of God). Does Christianity explain the complexities of human nature and experience? (It does because the Bible relates that, although the image of God and common grace enable us to do good to a certain extent, we are inclined to sin because of the Fall.)

This chapter has provided foundational principles for defending the faith. As we prepare to answer to our society regarding our faith, it is important that we learn to think logically, that we respond to the questions of our day, that we become familiar with the broad range of evidence at our disposal, and that we consider the person(s) we are addressing as we present our case. With these principles in mind, we strive to exhibit the truth of Jesus Christ in all of its splendor and, as always, leave the results to God.

2

Does God Exist?

Jimmy Williams

A fundamental matter concerning existence is the very existence at all of *something*. I am a part of some kind of reality. I possess a consciousness, an awareness that something is transpiring, unfolding, happening. You and I are part of it, and our observations and experiences inform us that we occupy a space-time universe that is characterized by a series of events. The intellect naturally asks, "What is this universe? From where did it come? Did the cosmos—that is, what we see—simply come into being from nothing, or has it always been here? Or is something or someone that transcends this material universe responsible for bringing it, and us, into existence?"

Metaphysical Options

All of these questions relate to the branch of philosophy called *metaphysics*. Webster defines *metaphysics* as "that division of philosophy which includes ontology, or the science of being and cosmology, or the science of fundamental causes and processes in things."[1] When we seek answers to the questions in the preceding paragraph, we are thinking metaphysically about the origin and the causes of the present reality. Regarding fundamental causes, few options can be cited to account for the existence of the universe. Three potential candidates are:

1. *Something came from nothing.* This view is widely rejected because the very idea defies rationality. Kenny remarks, "According to the big bang theory, the whole matter of the universe began to exist at a particular time in the remote past. A proponent of such a theory, . . . if he is an atheist, must believe that the matter of the universe came from nothing and by nothing."[2] Because by rules of logic (observation, causality), nothing cannot produce something, then something is eternal and necessary. Because any series of events is not eternal (thus a contradiction), there is, therefore, an eternal, necessary something that is not identical to the space-time universe.

2. *Matter is eternal* and capable of producing the present reality through blind chance. Carl Sagan was a proponent of this view: "All that ever was, all that is, and all that ever shall be is the Cosmos."[3] This second view has spawned two basic worldviews—*materialism* (or *naturalism*) and *pantheism.* Both hold the premise that nothing exists beyond matter. Materialism, therefore, is atheistic by definition. Pantheism is similar but insists that because God does not exist, nature is imbued with "God" in all of its parts.

3. *God created the universe.* This view, *theism,* asserts that Someone both transcends and did create the material universe of which we are a part. No other logical alternatives exist to explain the cosmos. Christians, along with all other theists, embrace this third view as the most reasonable explanation for what we find to be true of ourselves and of the world. Holding

this view is not simply a statement of blind faith; sound and rational reasons exist for adhering to the theistic view rather than the other two views. Theism is, therefore, a reasonable belief. In fact, it is more reasonable to believe that God exists than to believe that He does *not* exist. Theologians have posed several lines of "proof" to argue for God's existence. Although these arguments do not "prove" the existence of God, they do provide insights that may be used to show evidence of His existence.

The Cosmological Argument

The cosmological argument for the existence of God centers on the concept of causality. Every event and object, including the universe itself, has a cause. It has a beginning. A time existed when it was not and a time existed when it was. Hume states,

> An *infinite* number of real parts of time, passing in succession and exhausted one after another, appears so evident a contradiction that no man, one should think, whose judgment is not corrupted, instead of being improved, by the sciences, would ever be able to admit it.[4] (italics mine)

Hume is arguing here that time and space are *not* infinite and not eternal. Given that Hume's analysis is true, the universe—which is an effect—had a cause. And if the universe had a beginning, it is logical to suppose that it will have an end. Robert Jastrow comments,

> The most complete study made thus far has been carried out . . . by Allan Sandage. He compiled

information on 42 galaxies, ranging out in space as far as six billion light years from us. His measurements indicate that the universe was expanding more rapidly in the past than it is today. This result lends further support to the belief that the universe exploded into being.[5]

It also lends support to the idea that the universe may stop expanding. Jastrow adds,

> No explanation other than the big bang has been found for the fireball radiation. The clincher, which has convinced almost the last doubting Thomas, is that the radiation discovered by Penzias and Wilson has exactly the pattern of wavelengths expected for the light and heat produced in a great explosion.[6]

Jastrow also concludes that the universe is dying:

> Once hydrogen has been burned within that star and converted to heavier elements, it can never be restored to its original state. Minute by minute and year by year, as hydrogen is used up in stars, the supply of this element in the universe grows smaller.[7]
> Astronomers now find they have painted themselves into a corner because they have proven, by their own methods, that the world began abruptly in an act of creation to which you can trace the seeds of every star, every planet, every thing in this cosmos and on the earth. And they have found that all this happened as a product of forces they cannot hope to discover.[8]

Some people have argued that an *infinite regress* (the idea or claim that as one moves back in time, an endless procession of preceding moments will be encountered) of causes may not be logically possible. They say that the universe is not a "whole" that needs a single cause but rather is mutually dependent upon itself. Mutual dependence, however, misses the point, which is, Why does the universe exist rather than not exist? Reality and rationality suggest that every event has a cause. Likewise, whole series of events must have causes as well (because the whole is the sum of the parts). If all of the parts were taken away, would anything be left? If the answer is yes, then God exists (i.e., an eternal, necessary being that is more than the world). If the answer is no, then the whole is contingent, too, and needs a cause beyond it (God).

That God, then, does exist begs the most-often-asked question concerning the cosmological argument: From whence did God come? Although to ask this question of the universe, which we have just examined, is both reasonable and legitimate, to ask that same question of God is irrational and nonsensical because it invests Him with characteristics found in only the finite universe, which consists of space and time. By definition, something eternal must exist outside of space and time. The very question reveals the inquirer's fallacy of reasoning from within his or her own space-time context. God has no beginning; He *is!* (Exod. 3:14).

The Teleological Argument

The teleological argument for the existence of God addresses the order, complexity, and diversity of the cosmos. *Teleological* comes from the Greek word *telos*, which means "end" or "goal." The idea behind the teleological argument is that the observable order in the universe demonstrates that it is the end product of logic and that it functions according to an intelligent design, a fact that is obvious to an open-minded, intelligent being. The classic expression of this argument for intelligent design is the analogy of the watchmaker, which is found in William Paley's book *Evidences.* If we were walking on the beach and found a watch in the sand, Paley asserts, we would not assume that it washed up on the shore after having been formed through the natural processes and motions of the sea. Rather, we would naturally assume that it had been lost by its owner and that somewhere exists a watchmaker who originally designed and built it with a specific purpose in mind.

As the watch in Paley's argument is analogous to the universe, so the watchmaker is analogous to the One who is behind the intelligent design of the universe. Because intelligence cannot be produced by nonintelligence any more than nothing can produce something, there is, therefore, an eternal, necessary intelligence present and reflected in the space-time universe.

Until about five hundred years ago, humanity had no hesitation in acknowledging God as the Creator of the natural order. Most people perceived God to be the divine Designer, who created the universe with a purpose and maintained all things by the word of His power (Heb. 1:3; Col. 1:17). But the rise of modern science initiated the "demythologizing of nature," nature being the material world. Superstition and ignorance had ascribed spirit life even to forest, brook, and mountain. Things not understood scientifically were routinely accepted to be unexplainable, supernatural forces at work. Slowly, the mysterious, spiritual factor was drained away as scholars and scientists replaced it with natural explanations and theories of how and why things actually worked. After Copernicus, human significance diminished in the vastness of the cosmos, and people thought that only time and research, not God, were necessary finally to explain with accuracy the totality of the natural order. The idea of a transcendent One was deemed unnecessary, having been invalidated by the new theory of natural selection.

Ironically, the same science that took God away in recent centuries is creating the need to reconsider the possibility of His existence. Physics and quantum mechanics have now brought us to the edge of physicality, to a place where some people describe subatomic particle structures as spirit, ghostlike in quality. Neurophysiologists grapple with enigmatic observations suggesting that the mind transcends the brain. Psychology has developed an entirely new branch of study (parapsychology), which asserts that psychospiritual forces (ESP, biofeedback, etc.) actually function *beyond* the physical realm. Molecular biologists and geneticists, faced with the highly ordered and complex structures of DNA, ascribe to the chaining sequences a word that implies intelligence: the genetic *code.* And, as has been discussed already, astrophysicists have settled on the Big Bang theory of first cause, which seems to contradict the idea that matter is eternal. Rather, the universe, as huge as it is, seems to be finite.

Whether we look through the microscope or the telescope, to adhere to the old premise that such order and complexity are the products of blind chance becomes more difficult in the light of experimental science. Many of today's scientists have reexamined and challenged critically the old naturalistic assumptions and found them to be unconvincing by many of today's scientists. Dr. Walter

Bradley, Professor Emeritus of Mechanical Engineering at Texas A&M University, states the case:

> Discoveries of the last half of the 20th century have brought the scientific community to the realization that our universe and our planet in the universe are so remarkably unique that it is almost impossible to imagine how this could have happened accidentally, causing many agnostic scientists to concede that indeed some intelligent creative force may be required to account for it.[9]

Areas of reconsideration include cosmology and the origin of life; essential elements of design and their recognition; the minimal requirements for a universe to support life of any type and, specifically, complex human life; and why these requirements are met in our universe and why they are met uniquely by planet earth. All of these remarkable features of our world are being reevaluated and point toward intelligent design.

The Moral Argument

The moral argument for God's existence is based on the recognition of humankind's universal and inherent sense of right and wrong (cf. Rom. 2:14–15). No culture is without standards of behavior. All groups recognize honesty, wisdom, courage, and justice as virtues. And even in the most remote jungle tribes, murder, rape, lying, and theft are recognized as being wrong, in all places and at all times. The question arises, "From where does this sense of morality come?" C. S. Lewis, early in his classic work *Mere Christianity,* speaks of the origin of moral sense. He calls this moral law "The Rule of Right and Wrong . . . a thing that is *really there,* not made up by ourselves."[10] For years, Lewis struggled against God because to him the universe seemed unjust and cruel. But he began to analyze his outrage. Where did he get the very ideas of just and unjust? He said, "A man does not call a line crooked unless he has some idea of a straight line."[11]

Lewis suggests three areas in morality that are most likely to go wrong, and he uses the analogy of a fleet of ships on a voyage to demonstrate his point. First, ships may either drift apart or collide with and do damage to one another (analogous to alienation, isolation/people abusing, cheating, bullying one another). Second, individual ships may experience internal, mechanical breakdown (analogous to moral deterioration within an individual).[12] Here, Lewis points out a "catch 22": If the ships keep colliding they will not long remain seaworthy, and if their steering parts have been damaged in collision, they will not be able to avoid colliding. Third, the final part of morality that can go wrong concerns destination—"Where is the fleet of ships headed?" The voyage would be a failure if it were meant to reach New York but instead arrived in Buenos Aires (the destination analogous to the general purpose of human life as a whole, that for which man was made).

The human conscience, to which Paul refers in Romans 2, is not found in any other animal—only man. The utter uniqueness of this moral compass within humans, along with other exclusively human qualities (e.g., rationality, language, worship, and aesthetic inclinations), strongly suggests that man has not only a relationship *downward* to animals, plants, and earth but also a relationship *upward* to the God in whose image he is made. We addressed God's great power and intelligence in the cosmological and teleological arguments. Here, we argue that the human sense of morality, not known in the world of nature, finds its source in God's great righteousness. The Great Lawgiver's very character is the "straight line" (righteous, just, holy) against which all human actions are measured.

Atheism and Agnosticism

An atheist is a person who asserts, "There is no God." The statement is bold in that it expresses an absolute, and we have already established that the existence or nonexistence of God cannot be proven absolutely. The statement is also bold because to make such an assertion an atheist would literally have to be God. He or she would need to possess the qualities and capabilities to travel the entire universe, examining every nook and cranny, before arriving at such an unqualified, dogmatic conclusion.

The most brilliant, highly educated and widely traveled human on earth, having maximized his or her brain cells to optimum learning levels, could not possibly know one-one thousandth of all that could be known. And the pool of knowledge is doubling in mere years rather than in decades or centuries as in the past. Is it possible that God could still exist outside the very limited, personal knowledge/experience of one highly intelligent human being? Furthermore, an atheist must first acknowledge the concept of God so as to deny His existence.

The Bible says that "he who comes to God must believe that He is . . ." (Heb. 11:6). In other words, faith is necessary for one to believe in God's existence. But the preceding dogmatic and bold assertion is itself an expression of faith. It takes faith to believe that God *is,* and it takes faith to say that God *is not.* In fact, it might take even *more* faith for the atheist to believe in his or her position because an atheist holds to his or her faith against enormous amounts of evidence to the contrary. Christians also affirm God's existence on the basis of faith, but theirs is a reasonable—not a blind—faith that is based on the true nature of the cosmos.

Webster defines *agnosticism* as a position that states "neither the existence nor the nature of God, nor the ultimate origin of the universe is known or knowable."[13] Here again is a bold statement. When the agnostic says, "I don't know," the statement actually implies "I can't know, you can't know, and nobody can know."

Leith Samuel, in his little book *Impossibility of Agnosticism,* mentions the following three kinds of agnostics:

- The *dogmatic* agnostic says, "I don't know, you don't know, and no one can know." This type of agnostic already has his or her mind made up. He or she has the same problems as the atheist above who must know *everything* in order to hold this position with honesty.

- The *indifferent* agnostic says, "I don't know and I don't care." It is not likely that God would reveal Himself to someone who does not care to know: "He who has ears to hear, let him hear" (Luke 14:35).

- The *dissatisfied* agnostic says, "I don't know, but I would like to know." This person demonstrates an openness to truth and a willingness, given sufficient reason, to change his or her position. If such were the case, this type of agnostic would also be demonstrating what is true of agnosticism, namely, that it is meant to be a temporary path in search of truth, a path that gives way to a more reasonable and less skeptical view of life and all reality.[14]

For since the creation of the world His invisible

attributes, His eternal power and divine nature, have been clearly seen, being understood through what has been made, so that they are without excuse. (Rom. 1:20)

The fool has said in his heart, "There is no God." (Ps. 14:1)

3

The Problem of Evil

Rick Rood

Many people say that they do not believe in God because no loving God would allow evil and suffering among his creatures. Indeed, this is probably the most frequently raised objection to belief in God. John R. W. Stott has said, "The fact of suffering undoubtedly constitutes the single greatest challenge to Christian faith."[1] Even for the Christian, evil and suffering pose a severe test of one's faith in God.

Evidence of the fact of evil and suffering abounds. Earthquakes, floods, and disease cause immense suffering. Wars and acts of human treachery take their toll. The impact of these disasters is not limited to those who fail to love God. Believers experience every sort of evil experienced by nonbelievers. Why would a good and powerful God permit such circumstances? This is a question we cannot ignore. We must answer those who challenge our belief in God, just as we seek to live our lives as followers of Christ.

Christianity is not the only faith that struggles to answer questions about evil and suffering. Every system of belief (and unbelief) must address these issues. Pantheists, for instance, generally deal with the problem of evil in one of two ways: Evil is an illusion resulting from our state of ignorance about ultimate reality, or it actually finds its source in ultimate reality itself.[2] Evil as illusion hardly squares with our day-to-day experience of evil. If evil somehow finds its source in God, or any other kind of ultimate reality, we are left in moral confusion, and all hope is lost that evil might be overcome.

Dualists believe that good and evil coexist eternally. If this is the case, then God (who is good) is limited by eternal evil. A *limited* god is not God at all in any meaningful sense.

Atheists or naturalists see evil and suffering as simply part of the evolutionary process, a necessary reality. They resolve the tension between a world of evil and suffering and a God of power and love by negating God. They pay a high price for this negation, for they must be prepared to exist in a world without meaning. Again, there is no hope that evil and suffering will ever be overcome, other than by man's own ingenuity and perseverance. Is it any wonder that many atheists reach the point of abject despair? The atheist is confronted by an added dilemma: If there is no ultimate or absolute, there really is no objective standard for defining evil. Good and evil are meaningless concepts.[3]

But the focus of this chapter is on the problem posed by the existence of evil for the theist, and particularly for the Christian believer. How could a good and powerful God allow the evil we experience in our world? If He is all-powerful, it would seem that He can eliminate evil. If He is all-good or loving, it would seem that He wants to do so. But obviously He has not eliminated evil. So, how do we resolve this dilemma? Some theists modify the historically orthodox concept of God. They suggest God's power must be limited in some way, so that He is *not able* to eliminate evil.[4] This seriously compromises the biblical concept of the attributes of God. Scripture clearly testifies that He is unlimited in power. We will address the issue of God's power after we clarify the problem of evil itself.

Evil: Moral and Natural

To begin with, it is important for us to recognize that there are two broad classes, or types of evil: *moral* evil and *natural* evil. Moral evil results from the actions of free creatures, from individual murder, theft, or rape to the evil of entire peoples who wage immoral war. Natural evil results from natural processes, such as earthquakes and floods. Sometimes the two kinds of evil are intermingled, as when an earthquake results in more loss of human life than necessary because building contractors have cut corners or committed outright fraud in construction.

Evil: Philosophical Responses

Not only are there two *classes* of evil; there are two broad *approaches* to the problem of evil. One approach is the *philosophic* and *apologetic* approach, while the other is the *religious* or *personal* approach. The first approach addresses the issues raised by the skeptic who questions the possibility or the plausibility of the existence of a God who would allow the evil we see. Response to this challenge calls for the utilization of the tools of reason and evidence. The second approach confronts the issues raised by the believer whose faith in God is severely tested in the midst of personal suffering. In meeting this challenge, we must appeal to the truths revealed by God in Scripture.[5] We must address both the *logical* problem and the *evidential* problem. The logical problem asserts that it is *irrational* and hence *impossible* to believe in the existence of an all-good and all-powerful God. An all-good God *would* destroy evil, and an all-powerful God *could* destroy evil.

The key to resolving this "logical" problem is to recognize that whenever we say that God is "all-powerful" we are *not* saying that he can do anything whatsoever.[6] Scripture says that "with God all things are possible" (Matt. 19:26). But this does not mean that God can do anything conceivable. For example, Titus 1:2 tells us that God cannot lie. 2 Timothy 2:13 (NIV) tells us also that "he cannot disown [or be unfaithful to] himself." He always keeps his word. Neither can God be tempted to sin, nor can He tempt others to sin (James 1:13). So there obviously are exceptions to be acknowledged when we declare that God is "all-powerful" or able to do *all* things. He can do anything that is not contrary to his character as a holy, righteous God.

By inference, since God is a righteous God and also a *rational* being, neither can God do anything that is absurd or contrary to reason. For instance, God could not "undo the past," or "make a square circle."

We must conclude that, although God is certainly capable of destroying evil, it is impossible for Him to do so without at the same time rendering other purposes of his unachievable. And it would be irrational to expect that He could. For example, one of God's purposes is to fashion a race of human beings, created in His image, who are capable of entering into a genuinely loving relationship with Him. Yet, if human freedom were destroyed, such a loving relationship would be impossible. For freedom is the very essence of love. Love cannot be forced or coerced. Free creatures must be capable of choosing evil as well as good.[7]

Furthermore, God has purposes for His free human creatures that in fact *require* the existence of evil, specifically the development in human beings of genuine moral virtue.[8] We will consider this below. So, if it is indeed God's purpose to create human beings capable of entering into a loving relationship with Him, and if it is also His purpose to develop within them moral virtues which require the presence of evil, then it would be impossible for God to create a world in which evil does not exist.

The Natural By-Product

But what about natural evil? It seems apparent that God's purposes for human freedom and for moral virtue imply the inevitability of *moral* evil. But why must we also live in a world in which there are also many *natural* evils, such as disease, earthquakes, and floods? Scripture gives us some help at this point. First, it tells us that the world as it now exists is not the world as God made it. The New Testament comments on the natural effects of the fall of humanity into sin (Gen. 3:17–19) by noting that "the creation was subjected to frustration" (Rom. 8:20a NIV).

This is not to say that the world is no longer a wonderful place to live. It is still true that "the heavens declare the glory of God" (Ps. 19:1a NIV), and through God's good grace He provides for our needs and gives us many blessings to enjoy (Acts 14:17). The universe is still a *cosmos*, not a *chaos*. But it is true that much human suffering results from the effects of the Fall on creation. To some extent the natural order is subject to the actions of malevolent Satan and his demonic angels. This was evident, for example, in the experience of Job, who suffered greatly because of Satan's manipulation of the weather (see Job 1).

These facts would imply, then, that natural evil is in effect a *by-product* or *consequence* of moral evil![9]

Critics of this explanation raise some objections. First, couldn't God make free creatures who always love and obey Him? It is difficult to conceive how God could do this while preserving human freedom in its fullest sense. He could conceivably change our desires, choices, and actions by supernatural agency. But it seems difficult to see how beings whose desires, choices, and actions were under such control could be called free in any meaningful sense. Our relationship with God would not be genuinely and freely chosen.

Second, couldn't God miraculously intervene to prevent the evil consequences of human actions, or at least prevent evil from falling upon those who follow his will? Again, God could do these things, but not without virtually eliminating human freedom. If God allowed evil to befall only those who deserved it, people would turn to God simply to avoid suffering, or to experience His blessing. This would not be free choice. Also, if God's miraculous intervention were to become such a common occurrence, it is difficult to see how any reasonable person would disbelieve in Him. Free expression of personal choice would be lost.

Sheldon Vanauken said, "If only villains got broken backs or cancers, if only cheaters and crooks got Parkinson's disease, we should see a sort of celestial justice in the universe (but in that case, of course, no one would care to risk being a villain or a crook)."[10] God could not destroy evil in these ways without also seriously compromising human freedom, as well as the world in which free creatures now live and function.

The Evidential Problem of Evil

People who carefully evaluate the line of reasoning summarized in the previous section may choose not to accept it. Most will agree, however, that it adequately answers the logical challenge posed by belief in God's existence in light of the existence of evil. It is not irrational to believe that a good and loving God could *permit* evil, as a necessary consequence of His creation of free creatures who bear His image.

Skeptics contend that logical possibility is insufficient for faith. While it is *possible* that such a God would permit evil, the evidence of such great and seemingly purposeless evil makes God's existence highly *improbable*. In response, let us consider three observations.[11]

First, simply because we can *perceive* no purpose for evil does not mean no purpose exists for the spectrum and intensity of the evil we observe.[12] It is entirely possible that the reasons for much of the evil in our world are not only beyond our present knowledge; they may be beyond our capability of knowing. A child is not able to comprehend all the actions of his father. Neither should we expect to comprehend all the actions of an infinitely wise God (see Isa. 55:8; Rom. 11:33–36).

Second, we can conceive of *some* possible reasons God might allow evil into the world. Some people never sense a need for God apart from intense suffering. Perhaps there are purposes that God intends to accomplish among his angelic creation in the spiritual realm that would be impossible apart from the existence of suffering (cf. Job 1 and Eph. 3:10). Suffering may in some sense be preparatory to our existence in the life to come (2 Cor. 4:17).

Third, we must weigh the supposed improbability of God against all of the positive evidence that God exists and that Scripture gives a true account of reality. We cannot look only at the evidence of seemingly meaningless suffering. If we look at evidence, we must look at *all* exhibits—including the proofs for God and for Christ. Data to consider include the amazing design of nature, the proven historical reliability of the Bible, the fulfillment of messianic prophecy, and the documentation for the resurrection of Jesus Christ, as well as the examples of obvious personal transformation stemming from faith in God and Christ. On the basis of the *totality* of evidence, belief in a God who would permit the evil we see in our world is neither *unreasonable* nor *improbable*.

Evil: Religious Responses

We have looked at the philosophic/apologetic problem of evil, and the challenge of evil to our mind. But when we are experiencing the *effects* of evil in our own lives, we need more than intellectual reasons for our faith in God. This is especially true when the evil or suffering we experience appears to be undeserved or unjustified, and when we observe that those around us who *do* seem to deserve it are spared. This is the tension that inspired Asaph to pen Psalm 73. Under these circumstances, we need evidence from Scripture that God is One in whom we can not only believe, but One in whom we can also place our trust, and in whose love we can find our security. Again, some observations may help:

First, when we suffer it is not unnatural nor unspiritual to express its emotional pain. There are nearly as many psalms of lament in the Psalter as there are psalms of praise. The psalmist himself encourages us to "pour out your hearts" to God (Ps. 62:8 NIV).

Jesus Himself keenly felt the painful side of life. When

John the Baptist was beheaded, Jesus withdrew to a solitary place (Matt. 14:13), evidently to mourn. When Lazarus died, Christ knew that this was within the plan of God, nonetheless he openly wept at the grave of His good friend (John 11:35). In contemplating death on the cross, He suffered great anguish of soul (Matt. 26:38). It is not surprising that Jesus was called "a man of sorrows and acquainted with grief" (Isa. 53:3).

The apostle Paul likewise revealed something about his inner life when he confessed that the death of Epaphroditus would have caused "sorrow upon sorrow" in his heart. He considered Epaphroditus's continuing life a gift of God's mercy (Phil. 2:27).[13] There is for the Christian a capacity to experience both sorrow and joy, grief and hope, at the same time (see Paul's self-description in 2 Cor. 6:10, as "sorrowful, yet always rejoicing"). However, we do cross a line from sorrow to sin at the point when we allow grief to quench our faith in God, or lead us to accept the kind of counsel Job's wife gave him in the midst of his sufferings, to "curse God and die" (Job 2:9b).

Second, when we suffer we can draw comfort from the fact that God knows and cares about our situation and promises to be with us. Jesus reminds us that not a single sparrow is forgotten or unnoticed by God, and He goes on to say that we are of much greater value to Him than many sparrows (Luke 12:6–7).

Consider that "the LORD is close to the brokenhearted, and saves those who are crushed in spirit" (Ps. 34:18 NIV), and also that when we go through the "valley of the shadow of death," the Lord promises to be with us in this very place (Ps. 23:4). What a wonderful promise we are given in Isaiah 49:15–16a (NIV), "Can a mother forget the baby at her breast and have no compassion on the child she has borne? Though she may forget, I will not forget you! See, I have engraved you on the palms of my hands."

Consider also that God "does not willingly bring affliction or grief to the children of men" (Lam. 3:33 NIV), nor does He take pleasure in death (Ezek. 18:23, 32). Indeed, there is a sense in which God Himself suffers with His creatures. Speaking of the Lord's identifying with His people Israel, the prophet Isaiah said, "In all their distress he too was distressed" (Isa. 63:9a NIV). Jesus Himself showed the full range of human emotion. And it was He who said, "Anyone who has seen Me, has seen the Father" (John 14:9b NIV).[14]

We must consider that the very One upon whom we are invited to cast our anxieties is the One who cares for us (1 Peter 5:7).

Third, when we suffer we can draw great hope from the knowledge "that in all things God works for the good of those who love him, who have been called according to his purpose" (Rom. 8:28 NIV). This is not to say that all things (including evil things) are good. It is to say that, in a way beyond our comprehension, God is able to weave the darkest threads of life into the fabric of His good purposes for us. As Henri Blocher says, "Evil is conquered as evil because God turns it back upon itself."[15]

Because of this very fact, we are enabled to find joy in the midst of our trials (cf. Rom. 5:3–5; James 1:2–4), not because the trial itself is a cause for joy, but because in it God can find an occasion for producing godly virtues, and by it He can also promote His purposes in the world. This truth is not only stated in Scripture, but it is dramatically illustrated by the experience of Joseph. After years of unexplained suffering due to his brothers' maltreatment and betrayal, he could say to them: "You meant evil against me, but God meant it for good" (Gen. 50:20a). The supreme example of this principle, of course, is the death of Jesus Christ. Though an act of horrendous injustice, the Crucifixion was nonetheless the means used by God to provide for the redemption of the world. The greatest evil of all history became the means by which God accomplished the greatest good.

Consider some of the good things that can result from evil and suffering: It can provide an opportunity for God to display His glory, making evident His mercy, faithfulness, and love in the midst of painful circumstances (Rom. 8:31–39).

It can provide an opportunity for us to demonstrate love to others. "Carry each other's burdens, and in this way you will fulfill the law of Christ" (Gal. 6:2 NIV).

It can allow us to give proof of the genuine quality of our faith in God, and even serve to purify it (1 Peter 1:7), showing that we are faithful not simply for the benefits of God's blessing, but for the love of God Himself (Job 1:9–11).

Suffering can instill empathy and compassion, which enable us to better comfort others (2 Cor. 1:4). Consider that it was the sufferings of Christ that qualified Him to become our great High Priest, enabling Him to "sympathize with our weaknesses" (Heb. 4:15 NIV).

It can also deter us from sin, and motivate us to follow God more closely. Paul's "thorn in my flesh" kept him from undue pride, and engendered true humility and dependence on God (2 Cor. 12:7 NIV).

Suffering is also the teacher of obedience. Jesus was God Incarnate, yet as the Son "he learned obedience from what he suffered" (Heb. 5:8 NIV). Like us, as a man He learned by experience the value of submitting to the will of God His Father, even when it was the most difficult thing in the world to do.

Evil and suffering are necessary to the full development of such virtues as mercy and patience. Suffering can be a means of grace. How can we learn to show mercy and compassion, unless there is suffering and pain? How can we learn to be patient, unless the good we desire is delayed? How can we learn to extend grace and forgiveness to others, unless we experience injustice? Virtues such as these could never be fully realized in our lives, apart from the presence of evil.

Finally, when we suffer, a deep longing awakens within us for that day when God's purposes for permitting evil and suffering will be finally completed. Then we will be able to understand more fully. In the book of Revelation we are told that the day is coming when "He will wipe every tear from their eyes. There will be no more death or mourning or crying or pain, for the old order of things has passed away" (Rev. 21:4 NIV). The apostle Paul tells us: "Now we see but a poor reflection as in a mirror; then we shall see face to face. Now I know in part; then I shall know fully, even as I am fully known" (1 Cor. 13:12 NIV).

Those of us who have recognized our own sinful misuse of the gift of freedom and have received God's free gift of grace through Jesus Christ will at long last enter into that "best of all possible worlds" in the kingdom of God. Norman Geisler has persuasively argued that though this present world in which we live is certainly not the "best of all possible worlds," nonetheless it is the "best possible way to the best possible world." For in heaven we will have learned from experience the complete and tragic foolishness of turning away from God, and we will be granted the full vision of his goodness which will bind us freely and forever to Him.[16]

Afterwards

Light after darkness, gain after loss
Strength after weakness, crown after cross,
Sweet after bitter, hope after fears
Home after wandering, praise after tears
Sheaves after sowing, sun after rain,
Sight after mystery, peace after pain
Joy after sorrow, calm after blast,
Rest after weariness, sweet rest at last
Near after distant, gleam after gloom,
Love after loneliness, life after tomb
After long agony, rapture of bliss—
Right was the pathway leading to this.
—Frances R. Havergal[17]

Additional Reading

Blocher, Henri. *Evil and the Cross.* Trans. by David G. Preston. Downers Grove, Ill.: InterVarsity, 1994.

Carson, D. A. *How Long, O Lord? Reflections on Suffering and Evil.* Grand Rapids: Baker, 1990.

Clark, David K., and Norman L. Geisler. *Apologetics in the New Age: A Christian Critique of Pantheism.* Grand Rapids: Baker, 1990.

Craig, William L. *No Easy Answers: Finding Hope in Doubt, Failure, and Unanswered Prayer.* Chicago: Moody, 1990.

Crandall, Gary. *Gold Under Fire: The Christian and Adversity.* Winona Lake, Ind.: BMH, 1992.

Dobson, James. *When God Doesn't Make Sense.* Wheaton, Ill.: Tyndale House, 1993.

Feinberg, John S. *The Many Faces of Evil: Theological Systems and the Problem of Evil.* Grand Rapids: Zondervan, 1994.

Geisler, Norman L. *Philosophy of Religion.* Grand Rapids: Zondervan, 1974.

———. *The Roots of Evil.* Richardson, Tex.: Probe, 1989.

Geisler, Norman L., and Ronald M. Brooks. *When Skeptics Ask: A Handbook on Christian Evidences.* Wheaton, Ill.: Victor, 1990.

Kreeft, Peter. *Making Sense Out of Suffering.* Ann Arbor, Mich.: Servant, 1986.

Kushner, Harold S. *When Bad Things Happen to Good People.* New York: Avon, 1983.

Lewis, C. S. *The Problem of Pain.* New York: Macmillan, 1962.

Lloyd-Jones, Martyn. *Why Does God Allow Suffering?* Wheaton, Ill.: Crossway, 1994.

McGrath, Alister E. *Suffering and God.* Grand Rapids: Zondervan, 1992.

Nash, Ronald. *Faith and Reason.* Grand Rapids: Zondervan, 1988.

Peterson, Michael L., ed. *The Problem of Evil: Selected Readings.* Notre Dame, Ind.: University of Notre Dame Press, 1992.

Peterson, Michael, William Hasker, Bruce Reichenbach, and David Basinger. *Reason and Religious Belief: An Introduction to the Philosophy of Religion.* New York and Oxford: Oxford University Press, 1991.

Plantinga, Alvin C. *God, Freedom, and Evil.* Grand Rapids: Eerdmans, 1974.

Stott, John R. W. *The Cross of Christ.* Downers Grove, Ill.: InterVarsity, 1986.

Tada, Joni Eareckson, and Steven Estes. *When God Weeps: Why Our Sufferings Matter to the Almighty.* Grand Rapids: Zondervan, 1997.

Wenham, John W. *The Enigma of Evil: Can We Believe in the Goodness of God?* Grand Rapids: Zondervan, 1985.

Wiersbe, Warren W. *When Life Falls Apart.* Old Tappan, N.J.: Revell, 1984.

Yancey, Phillip. *Disappointment with God: Three Questions No One Asks Aloud.* Grand Rapids: Zondervan, 1988.

————. *Where Is God When It Hurts?* Grand Rapids: Zondervan, 1977.

4

Is Jesus the Only Savior?

Rick Rood

One of the most serious obstacles to the Christian faith is the claim that Jesus Christ is the exclusive Savior, the only way to God. In a society that places a high value on tolerance, such a claim draws the charge of being arrogant.[1] Yet, this claim of exclusivity is unavoidable, based on such well-known passages as these:

> Jesus answered, "I am the way and the truth and the life. No one comes to the Father except through me." (John 14:6 NIV)

> "Salvation is found in no one else, for there is no other name under heaven given to men by which we must be saved." (Acts 4:12)

How do we respond to the tension between these claims of exclusive salvation in Scripture and the reproach that such claims are arrogant and intolerant? Many propose, and some demand, that Christians trade their position on exclusivism for a more tolerant viewpoint. In this chapter we will examine two viewpoints that are proposed as alternatives to exclusivism.

Religious Pluralism

Religious pluralism is the view that all religions are equally valid ways to God.[2] Just as there are many paths up Mount Fuji, so there are many paths to God. In this view, the differences among religions are superficial. So long as they serve to bring people into contact with God (or "Ultimate Reality"), all religions are true vehicles of salvation.

The immediately apparent weakness of this view is that many differences among the beliefs and doctrines of the various religions are fundamental and irreconcilable with each other. They are mutually contradictory and sometimes bitterly antagonistic to one another.

Take, for example, the teachings of the major religions about the being of God. Hinduism espouses a generally pantheistic view of God, although many Hindus are practicing polytheists. Buddhism, as originally taught by Gautama Buddha, had no clear concept of God, though it developed into a pantheistic system. Islam is radically monotheistic to the point of being unitarian. Christianity is monotheistic but trinitarian. These views cannot all be true.

The teachings of the major religions about man and salvation are also mutually contradictory. Hinduism views human beings as essentially divine but trapped in the cycle of multiple reincarnations by ignorance and the law of *karma*. Deliverance comes through recognition of our true divine nature and atoning for our bad *karma*.

Buddhism is similar to Hinduism at this point but sees humans as trapped in this world of suffering by personal desire. Deliverance results from the elimination of all desire—ultimately even the desire to live. Islam teaches that, though people are weak in nature, they are able to keep

Allah's laws, and will suffer his judgment for disobedience. In Islam, people are not so much in need of a savior as in need of guidance.

Christianity teaches that every human being is under the judgment of a holy God, who cannot accept any sin into His presence. Salvation comes, not as the result of vain attempts to obey God's law perfectly, but as the result of God's gracious work through the atoning sacrifice of His Son, Jesus Christ, and by His Spirit who can change us from within.

It's apparent that the differences among the major religions are fundamental in nature. To suggest that all religions are true requires that we radically redefine the definition of "truth."

Some religious pluralists attempt to explain away these contradictions by distinguishing between *exoteric* (literal and obvious) *teaching* and the *esoteric* (hidden or mystical) *teaching* of the religions.[3] They claim that, although there are contradictions on the exoteric or literal level of doctrine, the deeper, mystical meaning is common to all religions at the esoteric level. The embracing of this mystical element leads to a common experience of the divine. But how can we really know that these experiences are all the same, or that they all lead to an encounter with the true God? If the real meaning of the teachings of Jesus (as an example) was really esoteric or hidden, His constant followers should have known it. But there is no hint, however, from the apostles that they believed this to be the case.

Many pluralists assert that what really matters is not the objective doctrinal teaching of a religion but the moral and spiritual transformation that occurs in the lives of followers.[4] However, genuine spiritual transformation is very difficult, if not impossible, for us to truly judge. Jesus strongly emphasized that true spiritual change takes place in the heart, not merely in external morality or religious piety (Mark 7:1–15). This kind of change only God can truly see and judge (Luke 16:15).

If religious pluralism asserts that all religions are in some sense true as they bring us into touch with God, we must conclude that in terms of what they objectively teach they are all false. They contradict each other in important ways at the objective level. It does seem improbable that false beliefs can guide us to a genuine experience of that which is true.

Certainly religious pluralism is problematic for the Christian, because it demands the rejection of the most foundational teachings of Scripture—the uniqueness and deity of Jesus Christ. Not only this, but it requires that all of the supporting evidence of prophetic fulfillment, the resurrection of Jesus Christ, and the witness of the apostles is irrelevant. It is no great wonder that religious pluralists spend a good deal of time attempting to undermine evidence of the trustworthiness of the Scriptures. If, however, the teachings of the Bible are true, then religious pluralism must be false, for the two are entirely incompatibile.

John Hick, one of the foremost contemporary proponents of religious pluralism, put it very well himself when he said, "For if Jesus was literally God incarnate, the Second Person of the Holy Trinity living a human life, so that the Christian religion was founded by God-on-earth in person, it is then very hard to escape from the traditional view that all mankind must be converted to the Christian faith."[5]

Christian Inclusivism

Orthodox Christians have not found the arguments for religious pluralism to be compelling. Yet at the same time, many Christians struggle with the seemingly rigid claims of exclusivism, and have therefore embraced the less radical view of *inclusivism*. Inclusivists believe that, although Jesus is the exclusive Savior, many who have not explicitly trusted in Him are included in His salvation, even among those who have not heard the gospel proclaimed.[6]

Inclusivists believe that God accepts an *implicit* faith in lieu of an explicit faith in Christ, when the latter is impossible. This may occur by a response to God's general revelation through creation or conscience, or to truth embedded in other religions.

First, inclusivists suggest that because people were saved apart from a full knowledge of Christ before He came, it must be possible for some to be saved in this way today. It is, of course, true that people who lived before the time of Christ did not know all that we know about Him. This does not, however, mean that people who lived before Christ knew nothing at all about God's work of salvation. Scripture makes it clear, that faith in God has always been necessary for salvation. "And without faith it is impossible to please God, because anyone who comes to him must believe that he exists and that he rewards those who earnestly seek him" (Heb. 11:6 NIV). From earliest times, salvation came to those who called "on the name of the LORD [Yahweh]" (Gen. 4:26b). Also, from the beginning there was revelation about the "seed" of the woman who would deliver humanity from the curse of sin (Gen. 3:15). Through the progressive revelation of the Old Testament, God taught about the Messiah and Savior to come. It seems apparent that people who came to God before the Christian era did indeed embrace by faith what had been revealed about the Messiah.

Of greater import to the inclusivists, however, are passages in the Old Testament that record the salvation Gentiles outside the covenant community of Israel. The two foremost examples of "pious Gentiles" are Melchizedek (Gen. 14:18-20) and Jethro (Ex. 2:16; 3:1), both of whom were said to be priests, though not a part of Israel. In the case of Melchizedek, it is clearly stated that he was a "priest of God Most High" (Gen. 14:18–20). It is likely that he came to this knowledge of God through the transmission of the original revelation to Adam and later to Noah and their descendants, although we cannot rule out direct divine revelation. It is also important to note that Abraham clearly identifies the God whom Melchizedek served as the "LORD" (Yahweh) in Gen. 14:22. In the case of Jethro, it is significant that he apparently came to an exclusive faith in the God of Israel through what he witnessed at the Exodus from Egypt. He confesses, "Now I know that the LORD is greater than all other gods" (Exod. 18:11). The fact that he had served as a priest in Midian really tells us nothing about his personal spiritual condition prior to coming to know the God of Israel in this fuller way. The faith of both these men appears to have been explicit.

Naaman the Syrian also is cited as an example of a believer outside Israel (2 Kings 5). His own words make it clear that he came to an explicit faith in the God of Israel through Elisha the prophet: "Now I know that there is no God in all the world except in Israel" (2 Kings 5:15 NIV). Furthermore, Naaman foresaw that when he returned to Syria he would be required to participate in temple observances in honor of the pagan god Rimmon, and he asked forgiveness in advance for these acts, which probably were an obligation of his military office. The impetus for this request was obviously based on his newly held assumption that it was wrong to worship such an idol.

The Ninevites who repented through the preaching of Jonah are also cited as believers outside the nation Israel. The book of Jonah does not state, however, that the Ninevites came to salvation. It merely states that they escaped God's immediate judgment, because they "believed God" (Jonah 3:5 NIV) and "turned from their evil ways" (3:10 NIV). Even if they did come to salvation, it was through the preaching of a Jewish prophet.

The Magi who came to worship the newborn Jesus are placed on the list of "pious Gentiles" (Matthew 2). It is clear, however, that, although their prior beliefs were no doubt pagan, they were seeking the true God and were guided to Jesus the Messiah in a remarkable way. They may have been familiar with the God of Israel through the prophecies of Daniel, a prophet who had served among the Magi in Babylon. They might also have had a record of the oracles of Balaam: "I see him, but not now; I behold him but not near; a star shall come forth from Jacob, a scepter shall rise from Israel" (Num. 24:17).

Cornelius the centurion is most often identified as an example of one who was one of God's own before hearing about Christ, even though he lived in the newly inaugurated Christian era. Indeed he is referred to as a "devout and God-fearing" man before ever hearing the gospel (Acts 10:2 NIV). Yet the book of Acts makes it clear that Cornelius did not receive salvation until Peter declared to him the message about Christ and the forgiveness of sins that comes through believing in him (10:43). In fact, the angel who prepared Cornelius for Peter's visit told him he would receive "a message through which you and all your household will be saved" (11:13–14 NIV).

In each of these examples, there is no evidence that any of them came into a saving relationship with God other than through explicit knowledge of and faith in Him. Once the nation Israel was established as a "kingdom of priests" among the nations (Exod. 19:6), every Gentile response of faith recorded in Scripture came through the agency of that nation. This is in accord with God's stated purpose that through the seed of Abraham all the nations would be blessed (see Gen. 12:3 and Psalm 67). This promise of international blessing motivated King Solomon to pray that, through the Lord's blessing of Israel, "all the peoples of the earth may know [His] name and fear [Him]" (1 Kings 8:43 NIV). Jesus himself said that "salvation is from the Jews" (John 4:22). This was the case until the establishment of the church as God's missionary agency in the world.

Beyond these biblical examples, however, inclusivists appeal to certain biblical texts.

Malachi 1:11 is sometimes quoted: "'My name will be great among the nations, from the rising to the setting of the sun. In every place incense and pure offerings will be brought to my name, because my name will be great among the nations,' says the LORD Almighty" (NIV). Inclusivists prefer to translate the verbs in this verse in the present tense (which is grammatically permissible), implying that people everywhere were worshiping the Lord, though without knowing the identity of the true God. In context, however, this is clearly a reference to the future, when the nations will be openly converted to the Lord. Zephaniah 2:11 agrees that "the LORD will be awesome to them when he destroys all the gods of the land.

The nations on every shore will worship him, every one in its own land" (NIV). It also fits with what the Lord said through Isaiah the prophet: "Turn to me and be saved, all you ends of the earth; for I am God, and there is no other" (45:22 NIV).

In Matthew 25:31–46, Jesus describes the basis on which He will judge the nations at His second coming. Will some be saved on the basis of their unconscious acts of love and compassion toward Jesus' "brothers" (v. 40)? Some point out that Jesus mentions nothing here about their faith in Him as their Savior. He mentions only their good works. This is seen as an indication that those who never heard the gospel will be judged on the basis of the fruitfulness of their "implicit" faith. That faith would have become explicit if they had been given the opportunity to hear and believe in the gospel.[7] But this is to misunderstand Jesus' intention in this chapter. Jesus is driving home the point that genuine believers will be characterized by such acts of kindness. Their faith will be shown by their works (cf. James 2:18). Actually, it is impossible that all of the people under consideration in this chapter will not have heard the gospel, because in the previous chapter Jesus said that the gospel would be "preached in the whole world as a testimony to all nations" (24:14). Those to whom the gospel will have been preached would certainly include those described by Jesus in this passage.

Jesus said in John 10:16, "I have other sheep that are not of this fold [the flock of believing Jews]." Inclusivists sometimes take this to refer to implicit believers outside the believing community. Notice, however, how Jesus proceeds to describe them: "I must bring them also. They too will listen to my voice, and there shall be one flock and one shepherd" (NIV). They will come into God's family by hearing and listening to the voice of the Lord. Jesus expands on how this will happen in His high priestly prayer of John 17: "My prayer is not for them alone [those who had already come to faith in Him]. I pray also for those who will believe in me through their message" (v. 20 NIV). This group includes the "other sheep," who hear the Shepherd by hearing and believing the gospel.

Peter's confession in Acts 10:34–35 is often quoted in support of implicit belief: "I now realize how true it is that God does not show favoritism but accepts men from every nation who fear him and do what is right" (NIV). Inclusivists argue that this passage shows that God provides salvation to people who fear God and seek to do what is morally right, apart from hearing and believing the gospel. But is this really what the passage says? This statement was made by Peter to reflect his newfound understanding that salvation is not for Jews only, as he had formerly believed. Rather, it is for all the world. Nationality is no barrier to God's acceptance. What inclusivists overlook is that God's acceptance toward the people described in this verse is manifest by His revealing to them the way of salvation, by sending the gospel to them that they might believe and be saved. This is reflected in the statement of the Jewish believers who heard Peter's account of Cornelius' conversion: "So then, God has granted even the Gentiles repentance unto life" (Acts 11:18 NIV). Cornelius is one of the "other sheep" that Jesus said he would bring into His flock (John 10:16). He was one of those who would believe through the message of the apostles (John 17:20).

In Acts 14:16–17 Paul stated that though in times past God had let the nations go their own way, yet He never had left the nations "without testimony: He has shown kindness by giving you rain from heaven and crops in their seasons; he provides you with plenty of food and fills your hearts with joy" (NIV). Some might take this to imply that, simply through responding to God's common grace and general revelation, people might come to know Him in a saving way. But this passage does not at all imply that this testimony to God's kindness is sufficient to bring salvation. Paul's point was that this testimony is sufficient to lead a person to seek the God of heaven, that he might know Him. This was what Paul and Barnabas had come to help their listeners do: "We are bringing you good news, telling you to turn from these worthless things (idols) to the living God, who made heaven and earth and sea and everything in them" (v. 15 NIV).

In Acts 17:23 Paul said that he had come to Athens to tell the Athenians about the God whom they worshipped in "ignorance" by constructing an altar "to an unknown God" (v. 23). He did not say, however, that this "ignorant worship" was sufficient to bring about their salvation. In fact, later in his Mars Hill Address he called upon them to "repent" (v. 30). The apostle's message to Jews and Gentiles alike was always that "they must turn to God in repentance and have faith in our Lord Jesus" (Acts 20:21 NIV). Indeed, in this very passage Paul states that God's intention was that those who lived in ignorance "would seek him and perhaps reach out for him and find him" (Acts 17:27 NIV).

Support for inclusivism is frequently also sought in the words of Paul in the first two chapters of his letter to the Romans, where he refers to the evidence for God in creation (Rom. 1:18–23), and to the voice of God in our conscience (2:14–16). Certainly, these two passages tell us that through creation it is possible to know that there is a Creator of eternal power and wisdom, and that through conscience it is possible to know that we deserve death, because our moral failings have alienated us from Him (1:32). But there is no indication here that these avenues of revelation are sufficient to bring a person into a saving relationship with God. Something more must be revealed to us if we are to be reconciled to Him.

This "something more" is defined in Romans 10:12–15a, 17 as the good news about Jesus Christ:

> For there is no difference between Jew and Gentile—the same Lord is Lord of all and richly blesses all who call on him, for, "Everyone who calls on the name of the Lord will be saved."
>
> How, then, can they call on the one they have not believed in? And how can they believe in the one of whom they have not heard? And how can they hear without someone preaching to them? And how can they preach unless they are sent? . . . Consequently, faith comes from hearing the message, and the message is heard through the word of Christ. (NIV)

The necessity of hearing and believing the gospel could not be more clearly stated.

This necessity is well illustrated in the many New Testament passages which describe this process in the lives of the first century believers. "I am not ashamed of the gospel, because it is the power of God for the salvation of everyone who believes: first for the Jew, then for the Gentile" (Rom. 1:16 NIV). "God was pleased through the foolishness of what was preached to save those who believe" (1 Cor. 1:21 NIV). "And you also were included in Christ when you heard the word of truth, the gospel of your salvation" (Eph. 1:13a NIV). "For you have been born again

. . . through the living and enduring word of God. . . . And this is the word that was preached to you" (1 Peter 1:23, 25b NIV). What other conviction could possibly have motivated the apostle Paul to declare,

> "I consider my life worth nothing to me, if only I may finish the race and complete the task the Lord Jesus has given me—the task of testifying to the gospel of God's grace. . . .
>   Therefore, I declare to you today that I am innocent of the blood of all men. For I have not hesitated to proclaim to you the whole will of God." (Acts 20:24, 26–27 NIV)

Paul says further, "It has always been my ambition to preach the gospel where Christ was not known, so that I would not be building on someone else's foundation. Rather, as it is written: 'Those who were not told about him will see, and those who have not heard will understand'" (Rom. 15:20–21 NIV).

Some Remaining Questions
Although the case for exclusivism is strong, some questions should be addressed.

> If Christianity is exclusively true, are other religions totally false?

No. There are truths in most religions. There are certainly some ethical truths in Buddhism and in Islam, for example. Islam even confesses belief in the God of Abraham. But there is no saving truth in any other religion, because they are based on a system of human works to achieve salvation. Chapter 15 will give a fuller analysis of this point.

> What about parallels to Christianity in other religions, like incarnations of God and sacrifices to God?

There are a few similarities to Christianity in some religions. But we must beware of drawing the conclusion that similarities imply equivalence. In no other religion is there provision of an atonement for sin through the sacrifice of the incarnate Son of God who gave proof of His deity by rising from the dead (see chap. 14). Even where there is sacrifice in other religions, the intent of the sacrifice is generally to provide sustenance to the god or to appease divine anger. The New Testament tells us that God Himself provides the sacrifice for our sin, out of His great love for the world (John 3:16). "Incarnations" in other religions are generally mythical appearances of a deity. Only in the New Testament do we find God assuming a human body and soul, and living a human life.[8]

> What, then is the source of other religions?

Other religions find their source in human reflection on the creation (Rom. 1:19–20), on moral consciousness (Rom. 2:14–15), and on a desire for immortality (Eccles. 3:11). This reflection, however, is distorted by the depraved human propensity to "suppress the truth" that can be known (Rom. 1:18, 21–23). The New Testament also tells us that Satan and his demons inspire false teaching (1 Timothy 4:1–3) and promote false righteousness (2 Cor. 11:13–15). Close parallels to Christianity in other reli-

gions sometimes result from contact with the Jewish and
Christian Scriptures. This is certainly true of Islam.

What about the possibility of coming to faith in Christ after death?

Most inclusivists (and even some exclusivists) find the
idea attractive that unbelievers will have an opportunity
to respond to the gospel after death. Support for this view
generally is sought in the statements in 1 Peter 3:19 and
4:6, which refer to Jesus' preaching to "the spirits in prison"
(3:19 NIV) and to the preaching of the gospel "even to
those who are now dead" (4:6). A close examination of
these texts in their contexts shows that in the first instance (3:19) the proclamation was one of judgment rather
than salvation. In the second (4:6) Peter is referring to the
proclamation of the gospel to those who had previously
heard him but were now no longer living. At the time of
Peter's writing, these people were now dead.[9] Furthermore,
the idea that people can be converted after death appears
clearly to be denied by Hebrews 9:27: "Man is destined to
die once, and after that to face judgment" (NIV).

What is the fate of those who never hear the gos-pel during their lifetimes?

Scripture tells us that God "rewards those who earnestly
seek him" (Heb. 11:6 NIV). It also tells us that it is God's
intention that men and women be prompted to seek Him
as a result of the testimony or witness He has given to all,
through his creation and providential guidance of the
natural order (see Acts 14:17 and 17:27). From these two
facts alone, it would seem fair to conclude that God will

reward with fuller revelation the person who responds to general revelation and to the prompting of the Holy Spirit by seeking God (see Jer. 29:13). This principle is behind the statement of Jesus in Luke 8:18, "Therefore take care how you listen; for whoever has, to him shall more be given." That is, the person who welcomes the revelation he has, will be given more. This principle is illustrated by the Ethiopian eunuch in Acts 8:26-40 and by Cornelius in Acts 10. These two God-fearing Gentiles had responded to what they knew of God, and the Lord went to great lengths to see that they received the gospel. This is God's normal way of salvation. Though it is not at all impossible that He has revealed the truth of the gospel to some in extraordinary ways apart from human agency, we are clearly told that His normal way is to send it by a human messenger (Rom. 10:14–15). It is this truth which lies behind our Lord's commission to "Go into all the world and preach the good news to all creation" (Mark 16:15 NIV). And it is to this commission that we should give our lives!

> And thus I aspired to preach the gospel, not where Christ was already named, . . . but as it is written, "They who had no news of Him shall see, and they who have not heard shall understand." (Rom. 15:20–21)

> For "whoever will call upon the name of the Lord will be saved." How then shall they call upon Him in whom they have not believed? And how shall they believe in Him whom they have not heard? And how shall they hear without a preacher? (Rom. 10:13–14)

Additional Reading

Anderson, Norman. *Christianity and World Religions: The Challenge of Pluralism.* Downers Grove, Ill.: InterVarsity, 1984. This is an excellent discussion of the uniqueness of Christianity in contrast to other major religions. Anderson presents the inclusivist position in chapter 5.

Boa, Kenneth, and Larry Moody. *I'm Glad You Asked.* Colorado Springs, Colo.: Chariot Victor, 1994. See chapters 8 and 9 on world religions and the question of the unevangelized.

Clarke, Andrew, and Bruce Winter. *One God, One Lord.* Grand Rapids: Baker, 1992. This book provides a serious discussion of the biblical perspective on other religions.

Fernando, Ajith. *The Christian's Attitude toward World Religions.* Wheaton, Ill.: Tyndale, 1987. A helpful discussion of the biblical case for exclusivism.

House, Paul R., and Gregory A. Thornbury, eds. *Who Will Be Saved? Defending the Biblical Understanding of God, Salvation, and Evangelism.* Wheaton, Ill.: Crossway, 2000. This is an excellent discussion of the issues identified in the title.

Nash, Ronald H. *Is Jesus the Only Savior?* Grand Rapids: Zondervan, 1994. A reasoned response to the pluralist and inclusivist positions by a convinced exclusivist.

Netland, Harold A. *Dissonant Voices.* Grand Rapids: Eerdmans, 1991. A scholarly rebuttal of the pluralist viewpoint.

Okholm, Dennis L., and Timothy R. Phillips, eds. *More than One Way? Four Views on Salvation in a Pluralistic World.* Grand Rapids: Zondervan, 1995. Chapters are contributed by proponents of the pluralist, inclusivist, and particularist (exclusivist) viewpoints.

Piper, John. *Let the Nations Be Glad! The Supremacy of God in Missions.* Grand Rapids: Baker, 1993. Chapter 4 contains an excellent discussion of the necessity of faith in Christ for salvation.

Richard, Ramesh P. *The Population of Heaven.* Chicago: Moody, 1994. An informed refutation of the inclusivist position.

Rommen, Edward, and Harold Netland, eds. *Christianity and the Religions: A Biblical Theology of World Religions.* Pasadena, Calif.: William Carey Library, 1995. A very helpful discussion of the biblical material concerning other religions.

Sanders, John. *What About Those Who Have Never Heard? Three Views on the Destiny of the Unevangelized.* Downers Grove, Ill.: InterVarsity, 1995. Chapters are written by advocates of inclusivism, universalism, and restrictivism (exclusivism).

5

Apologetics and Evangelism

Jimmy Williams

Today, as never before, Christians are being called upon to give reasons for the hope that is within them. Often, in the evangelistic context, seekers raise questions about the validity of the gospel message. Removing intellectual objections will not make one a Christian; a change of heart wrought by the Spirit is also necessary. That intellect alone is insufficient to bring another to Christ does not mean that it is unnecessary. This chapter examines the place and purpose of apologetics in sharing our faith with others.

The word *apologetics* never actually appears in the Bible. But at least one verse contains its meaning: "Sanctify Christ as Lord in your hearts, always being ready to make *a defense* to everyone who asks you to give an account for the hope that is in you, yet with *gentleness* and *reverence*" (1 Peter 3:15, italics added).

The Greek word *apologia* means "answer," or "reasonable defense." It does not mean to apologize, nor does it mean merely to engage in intellectual dialogue. It means to provide reasonable answers to honest questions and to do it humbly, respectfully, and reverently. Thus, the preceding verse suggests that the *manner* in which one presents apologetics is as important as the content. And Peter tells us in this passage that Christians are to be ready *always* with answers for those who inquire of us concerning our faith. Most Christians need a great deal of study before they can apply this verse in their evangelistic efforts.

Several questions often arise in a discussion about the merits and place of apologetics. What is the relationship of the mind to evangelism? Does the mind play any part in the process? What about the effects of the Fall? Isn't man dead in trespasses and sins? Doesn't the Bible say that we are to know nothing among men except Jesus Christ and Him crucified? Why do we have to get involved at all in apologetics if the Spirit is the One who actually brings about the new birth?

Many Christians are convinced that answering the intellectual questions of unbelievers is a waste of time. These Christians believe that any involvement of the mind in the gospel interchange smacks too much of human effort and dilutes the work of the Spirit.

But Christianity thrives on intelligence, not ignorance. If a real reformation is to accompany the revival for which many of us pray, it must be of the mind as well as of the heart. Jesus said, "Come, and you will see" (John 1:39); He thus invites our scrutiny and investigation both before and after conversion. We are to love God with the mind as well as with the heart and the soul.

Note that the writings of the earliest church fathers, up to the time of Constantine (A.D. 312), reflect Jesus' teaching in regard to the mind, heart, and soul. Before Constantine, beginning with Nero (A.D. 45–68), Christians endured severe persecution at the hands of the various Caesars for 250 years. During this period of persecution, the early fathers had their hands full answering their critics, both from inside (sects and heresies) and outside (pagans and Jews) the fledgling church. Thus, the first theology of the early church was apologist, that is, giving reasons for the belief that they had. The church did not even address such cardinal doctrines as the Trinity or the divine nature of Christ until after Constantine became emperor.

The early church was powerful and successful because of the depth of its commitment and its resolve to suffer and die for the gospel message in a hostile environment. But its dramatic impact occurred, too, because it out-thought and out-loved the ancient world. We seem not to be doing either very well today. And like the people in the early church, we, too, are under siege from prevailing cultural thought that is increasingly hostile to and skeptical of our cherished beliefs. But unlike the people in the early church, we are largely failing at the tasks of loving and thinking, which were so powerfully carried forth by the early church.

Reasoning and Persuading

Most Christians today seem to prefer *experiencing* Christianity to *thinking* about or *explaining* it. But consider the following verses:

> Matthew 13:23: "And the one on whom seed was sown on the good soil, this is the man who hears the word and *understands* it; who indeed bears fruit" (italics added). They all *heard* it, but only the "good soil" *comprehended* it.

> Acts 8:29–31: "And the Spirit said to Philip, 'Go up and join this chariot.' And when Philip had run up, he heard him reading Isaiah the prophet,

and said, 'Do you *understand* what you are reading?' And he said, 'Well, how could I, unless someone *guides* me?'" (italics added).

Acts 18:4: Paul at Corinth was "reasoning in the synagogue every Sabbath and trying to *persuade* the Jews and Greeks" (italics added).

Acts 19:8: Paul at Ephesus "entered the synagogue and continued speaking out boldly for three months, *reasoning* and *persuading* them about the kingdom of God" (italics added).

Romans 10:17: "So faith comes from *hearing,* and *hearing* by the word of Christ" (italics added). Again, the emphasis is on hearing with perception.

2 Corinthians 5:11: "We *persuade* men," says Paul (italics added). Vine's *Expository Dictionary* translates the Greek word for *persuade* as "to apply persuasion, to prevail upon or win over, bring about a change of mind by the influence of reason or moral considerations."[1]

All of these words—*persuasion, dialogue, discourse, dispute, argue, present evidence, reason with*—are vehicles of communication and are at the heart of Paul's classical evangelistic model. Can saving faith exist without understanding? Can understanding exist without reasoning? The Bible appears to say no.

J. Gresham Machen, a great Christian scholar, expressed the following to a group of young men at Princeton Seminary in 1912:

It would be a great mistake to suppose that all men are equally well-prepared to receive the Gospel. It is true that the decisive thing is the regenerative power [of the Holy Spirit] in connection with certain prior conditions for the reception of the Gospel. . . . I do not mean that the removal of intellectual objections will make a man a Christian. No conversion was ever wrought by argument. A change of heart is also necessary . . . but because the intellectual labor is insufficient, it does not follow that it is unnecessary. God may, it is true, overcome all intellectual obstacles by an immediate exercise of His regenerative power. Sometimes He does. But He does so very seldom. Usually He exerts His power in connection with certain conditions of the human mind. Usually He does not bring into the kingdom, entirely without preparation, those whose mind and fancy are completely contaminated by ideas which make the acceptance of the Gospel logically impossible.[2]

If these words were true in 1912, how much more should we heed them today?

Individual Response: Motivation and Mind Set

People respond to the gospel for various reasons—some out of pain or a crisis and others out of emotional needs such as loneliness, guilt, insecurity. Some people respond out of fear of divine judgment. And coming to know Christ brings a process of healing and hope. To know Christ is to find comfort for pain, understanding for insecurity and low self-esteem, and forgiveness for sin and guilt.

But other people have intellectual questions that block their acceptance of the Christian message. Some skeptics, if they are exposed to the proper information, do find in Christ the answers to their intellectual doubts and questions. Those who are currently involved in evangelism recognize the need to present such information when witnessing to certain people, and many more people express doubt and skepticism today than even twenty years ago.

We can see more clearly where we are as a culture by looking at Paul's world in the first century. Christianity's early beginnings flourished in a Graeco-Roman culture that was even more X-rated and brutal than our own. And we find Paul adapting his approach from group to group. He expected, for instance, to find certain attitudes when he approached the Jewish communities and synagogues from town to town. He knew that he would encounter a group that already held certain beliefs that were not in contradiction to the gospel that he preached. Such Jewish communities were strict monotheists; they believed in one God. They also believed that this God had spoken to them in their Scriptures and had given them absolute moral guidelines for behavior (the Ten Commandments).

But when Paul went to the Gentile community, he had no such expectations. He knew that there he would face a much different culture, one that was polytheistic (worshiping many gods), biblically ignorant, and living perverted, wicked lifestyles. And when he preached the gospel on Mars Hill in Athens, Paul adapted his presentation in light of their culture and mind-set. He spoke of God in terms of His presence and power, and he even quoted a Greek poet: "We also are [God's] offspring" (Acts 17:28).

One hundred years ago, the vast majority of Americans

reflected the first-century Jewish mentality, believing in God, having a basic respect for the Bible, and holding strong convictions about what is right and wrong. We can still find such Americans today, but a Gallup poll reveals that those Americans aren't having much of an impact on the pagan, or Gentile, community, which holds few beliefs that are compatible with historic Christianity. To evangelize such people, we have our work cut out for us. And we will have to use both our minds and our hearts to "become all things to all men, that [we] may by all means save some" (1 Cor. 9:22).

Three Inadequate Approaches

Many people do not share our Christian view of the world, and some of them are openly hostile to it. In fact, a college professor recently commented that the greatest impediment to social progress right now is the bigoted, dogmatic Christian community. That's you and me. This professor suggests that if we could just loosen up a little and compromise on some issues, America would be a happier place. This view means not just tolerance but wholesale acceptance of any lifestyle and personal choice. But the Bible calls us to be salt and light in the world. How can we effectively do that? I don't have all of the answers, but from more than forty years in active ministry, I will tell you what *isn't* working. Far too many Christians are addressing the critical issues of our day with one of the following three ineffective approaches.

Defensive. Many Christians are focused on and preoccupied with the issues of the strength of our defenses and the height of our walls. This "barricade mentality" has resulted in a Christian subculture. We have our own language, literature, heroes, music, customs, and educational systems. We certainly need places of support and fellowship. But when Paul describes spiritual warfare in 2 Corinthians 10:3–5, he depicts the enemy as being the ones behind walls, inside strongholds of error and evil. And Paul depicts the Christians as those who should be mounting offensives against these walls, tearing down the "lofty thing raised up against the knowledge of God" (v. 5) We are to be *taking* ground, not just defending and holding it.

Defeatist. Other Christians have given up. "Things are so bad," they say, "that my puny efforts won't change anything. After all, we are living in the last days, and Jesus said that things would just get worse and worse."

This point might be true, but it might not. Jesus said that no man knows the day or the hour of His coming. Martin Luther said, "If Jesus were to come tomorrow, I'd plant a tree today and pay my debts." The coming of the Lord may well be near, but He could also tarry a while. Because we don't know for sure, we should be preparing ourselves and our children to live for Him in the twenty-first century.

Devotional. Other Christians try to say something about their faith, but they can share only their personal religious experience. It is true that Paul speaks of us an epistle, or "letter, . . . known and read by all men" (2 Cor. 3:2). Our life/experience with Christ is a valid witness. But others have experienced "changed" lives, too, and Jesus didn't do the changing. Therefore, evangelism today must be something more than swapping experiences. We must learn how to ground our faith in the facts of history and the claims of Christ. We must seek ways to get people face to face with Jesus Christ so they can grapple with Him and not just acknowledge our experience of Him.

Rethinking Evangelism Efforts

We must remember a number of important principles as we share our faith with those who need Christ.

Broaden the concept of evangelism. When does evangelism actually occur? Many people perceive evangelism to be only the formal, final presentation of the gospel to an individual. But Jesus saw a much broader process: "Already he who reaps is receiving wages, and is gathering fruit for life eternal; that he who sows and he who reaps may rejoice together. For in this case the saying is true, 'One sows, and another reaps.' I sent you to reap that for which you have not labored; others have labored, and you have entered into their labor" (John 4:36–38).

Christians should rejoice over—to mix metaphors—a "five-yard spiritual gain" in someone's life. Soil preparation, sowing, watering, and reaping are all part of the evangelistic process. The Bible knows nothing of "pre-evangelism." It speaks of only two terms to describe the human condition: *lost* and *found.* Everyone who is lost needs Christ and the new birth. Evangelism includes everything that leads toward that event in a person's life. And once a person experiences the new birth, a second process begins—the discipling and spiritual development of that individual from "babe" to "young man" or "young woman" to "mature believer."

The intellectual comprehension of the Christian faith must be deepened. As was already stated, the Bible admonishes us to love God with the mind, to be transformed by renewing our mind and thinking "Christianly" about life as a whole. But the Bible also instructs, "Study to shew thyself approved unto God, a workman that needeth not to be ashamed, rightly *dividing* the word of truth" (2 Tim. 2:15 KJV, italics added). Today's Christians are prone to look elsewhere than the Word to deepen their understanding of their faith, preferring Christian fiction, "self-help" books, devotional literature, and missionary biographies. Indeed, a place exists for such literature in the lives of believers. But Paul reminds us in the preceding passage that we are to *know* what we believe. Every Christian should be building a reservoir of knowledge and experience upon which the Spirit can draw when opportunities for evangelizing present themselves. Jesus is the model in this regard; we find Him in the Gospels fully prepared for ministry to diverse peoples.

Admit the limitations of our knowledge. Christians do not have final answers to all questions. The limits of our knowledge are twofold. First, we are limited in what we know of truth in general. Note that George Washington died probably ten or fifteen years before he otherwise might have died because, being the first president, he received the best medical attention of the day! The cutting edge of medical technology in the late eighteenth century called for bleeding the patient with leeches. This repeated procedure so weakened Washington's body that he died. Two hundred years later, our generation knows much more about life and the universe, but it is also important to remember that human beings don't *invent* truth; they only *discover* it. God invites man to explore that which He created: "Let them rule . . . over all the earth. . . . Be fruitful and multiply, . . . and subdue it" (Gen. 1:26–28). We have advanced far beyond colonial technology, but we have just begun to explore and understand all there is to know about what is true in the universe. Sometimes Christians must leave things in tension, let the dialogue continue, and wait for more evidence.

The second limitation to our understanding concerns

revealed truth. It is likely that God, who has spoken, has not revealed to us all that could be known. A further challenge in determining God's revelation concerns the Bible itself. What does a word or a passage really say? Michelangelo, the great sculptor and painter of the Renaissance, was commissioned to create a statue of Moses. At the time, understanding of the Bible reflected Moses, after coming down from communing with God on Mt. Sinai, as having horns upon his head! To be true to the Scriptures, Michelangelo carved a set of horns on Moses' head, and thousands of tourists see them every day at St. Peters in Vincoli, Rome. In Michelangelo's day, scholars thought that the Hebrew word *keren* meant "antler" or "horn." But later scholars discovered that the word could also mean "ray of light," "point," or "peak." The error was not with God's revelation in the Bible but in man's understanding of the meaning of the word.

Let this illustration caution Christians against making dogmatic assertions. Certainly, some things within a Christian worldview should be consider nonnegotiable. Regarding *justification by faith*, for example, the biblical evidence is too strong to consider alternatives. But in regard to issues such as the age of the earth, the time and nature of Christ's return, whether man should explore space, and a host of other matters over which godly men and women disagree, Christians would do well to leave things in tension. History is witness to Christians who, convinced of biblical support, have gotten out on the end of some theological limb, only to have someone saw it off behind them.

Develop a complete apologetic. This point involves one's *ethics,* one's *emotional connection,* and one's *logical presentation.* The ethical dimension concerns the credibility of the witness. Does he or she reflect genuineness? Does his or her demeanor and character represent Jesus Christ, or does the witness send mixed messages about what he or she says and who he or she is? The more powerful the personal aspect, the greater potential for effect. You and your experience with the Lord are a vital ingredient of your witness.

The emotional dimension involves caring and relationship. It is possible to be direct and proactive with people while still treating them with integrity. It is important that hearts as well as heads meet and that one possesses the capacity to identify with a hurting or confused person.

The logical dimension involves the presentation of evidence and argument. Take care not to offer more information than is needed. And for those who resist or reject reasonable answers, be aware that the person's motive for doing so might not be intellectual at all, but rather moral, that is, a problem of the will.

Take them to Jesus. When Philip witnessed of Christ to Nathanael, the latter questioned whether any good thing (prophet) could come out of Nazareth (John 1:46). Philip didn't have a ready answer, so he took Nathanael to Jesus. Christians should do the same when we are "in over our heads" and lack answers. All of the answers we offer ultimately funnel down to the place where the person whom we are trying to reach is face to face with Christ and His unique claims. Jesus said, "And I, if I be lifted up from the earth, will draw all men to Myself" (John 12:32).

Remember—apart from God's Spirit, no one would ever be converted. No matter how effective the human efforts, it is not possible for any person to see and embrace the gospel of Jesus Christ without divine enablement (John 6:44). God has told us to go and tell. We do the going and telling, and the Spirit does the saving. Can God use a dull tool? Of course He can. But He can use a sharpened tool much more effectively. It is the privilege and the responsibility of every Christian to go and tell, to make every effort to be as sharp an instrument as possible for the glory of God.

Essentials for Effective Evangelism

We must remember some important practices if we Christians want to be effective in bringing others to Christ through our individual witness.

Go to people. The heart of evangelism is Christians taking the initiative to "fish for men." Acts 17:17 describes how Paul was effective in his day and time: "He was reasoning in the synagogue with the Jews and the God-fearing Gentiles, and in the market place every day with those who happened to be present."

Communicate. Engage your listeners. Sharing the gospel involves communication. People must be focused upon and understand the gospel to respond to it. Our responsibility as Christians is to make the gospel message as clear as possible for all who will listen: "Therefore knowing the fear of the Lord, we persuade men" (2 Cor. 5:11).

Relate. Effective witness involves not only transmitting biblical information but also establishing a relationship with other persons. Hearts, as well as heads, must meet. "Having thus a fond affection for you," Paul wrote to the Thessalonians, "we were well-pleased to impart to you not only the gospel of God but also our own lives, because you had become very dear to us" (1 Thess. 2:8).

Remove barriers. Part of our responsibility involves having the skills to eliminate obstacles, real or imagined, that keep an individual from taking the Christian message seriously. When God sent the prophet Jeremiah forth, He said, "Behold, I have put My words in your mouth. See, I have appointed you . . . to pluck up and to break down, to destroy and to overthrow, to build and to plant" (Jer. 1:9–10). Sometimes our first task is one of spiritual demolition, removing derelict assumptions and preconceptions, then breaking up hard ground to prepare a highway for God in someone's life.

Explain the gospel. We need an army of Christians today who can consistently and clearly present the message to as many people as possible. Luke says of Lydia, "The Lord opened her heart to respond to the things spoken by Paul" (Acts 16:14). This brief passage presents four essential elements that are present every time the gospel is shared:

1. someone talking (Paul),
2. something spoken (gospel),
3. someone listening (Lydia), and
4. the Lord opening the heart.

Invite others to receive Christ. Our presentation can be clear but still ineffective if, after sharing the gospel with someone, we fail to give them the opportunity and encouragement to take that first step of faith. Paul's words encourage us to do so: "Therefore, we are ambassadors for Christ, as though God were entreating through us; we beg you on behalf of Christ, be reconciled to God" (2 Cor. 5:20).

Make every effort by every means to establish new believers in the faith. After someone has taken that step, maintain relationship with that person, grounding him or her in the Scripture, helping that person gain assurance of salvation, and helping him or her get active in a fellowship at a church that honors Christ and teaches the Bible: "Not forsaking our own assembling together, as is the habit of some, but encouraging one another" (Heb. 10:25).

Part 2

The Bible

6

Are the Biblical Documents Reliable?

Jimmy Williams

How do we know that the Bible we have today is even close to the original? Haven't copiers down through the centuries inserted and deleted and embellished the documents so that the original message of the Bible has been obscured? These questions are frequently asked in an attempt to discredit the information revealed in Scripture.

Errors to Avoid

In responding to the preceding questions, first, do not say, "We know that the Bible is inspired and infallible because the Bible itself says so." You will be accused of using circular reasoning.

Second, when considering the original documents, disregard the present form of your Bible and perceive it for what it is—a collection of copies of ancient source documents.

Third, do not start with modern "authorities" and then

move to the documents to see if the authorities were right. Begin by testing the documents themselves for validity.

Procedure for Testing a Document's Validity

In his book *An Introduction to Research in English Literary History,* C. Sanders establishes three tests of reliability that are employed in general historiography and literary criticism: *bibliographical* test (i.e., the textual tradition from the original document [the autograph] to the copies and manuscripts of that document we possess today), *internal* evidence (what the document claims for itself), and *external* evidence (information in the document must agree with known historical facts, dates, persons from its own contemporary world). Sanders is a professor of military history, not a theologian, and he uses these three tests of reliability in his own study of historical military events.[1] Similarly, this chapter focuses upon the bibliographical, or textual, evidence for the Bible's reliability.

The Old Testament

For both the Old and New Testaments, the question is "Because none of the original copies—or even scraps—of the Bible survive, are the oldest extant manuscripts we *do* have reliable enough for us to reconstruct biblical documents that give us a true, undistorted view of actual people, places, and events?"

The Scribe

When considering the Old Testament documents, one must take into account the caliber of the people who did the copying. In antiquity, no printing presses existed, so people called *scribes* were trained to copy documents. The scribe, usually a devout Jew, was considered a professional.

Scribes believed that they were working with the very Word of God and, therefore, practiced extreme care in copying. They did not jot things down hastily.

The Massoretic Text

The earliest complete copy of the Hebrew Old Testament dates from about A.D. 900. During the early part of the tenth century, a group of Jews called the Massoretes existed. These Jews were meticulous in their copying, working from texts that were in all-capital letters, with no punctuation or paragraphs. The Massoretes would copy Isaiah, for example, and when they were through, they would calculate the number of letters. They would then count to the middle letter of the book. If it was not the same, they made a new copy. All of the extant copies of the Hebrew text that come from this period are in remarkable agreement. Comparisons of the Massoretic text with earlier Latin and Greek versions have also revealed that great care was taken in copying and that little deviation occurred during the thousand years from 100 B.C. to A.D. 900. But until this century, scant material from antiquity written in Hebrew existed that could be compared with the Massoretic texts of the tenth century A.D.

The Dead Sea Scrolls

In 1947, a young Bedouin goatherd found some clay jars in caves near the valley of the Dead Sea. Inside the jars were scrolls on papyrus, leather, and copper. The discovery of the Dead Sea Scrolls at Qumran has been hailed as the outstanding archeological discovery of the twentieth century. The scrolls revealed that a commune of monastic farmers flourished in the valley from 150 B.C. to A.D. 70. Most scholars have concluded that this community was that of the *Essenes,* of whom three first-century scholars—Josephus (A.D. 37–100), Philo (20 B.C.–A.D. 50), and Pliny (A.D. 61–113)—spoke. Scholars believe that when the Romans invaded the land, the Qumran community put their cherished scrolls in the jars and hid them in the caves on the cliffs northwest of the Dead Sea. Because these scrolls were never reclaimed, archaeologists have concluded that the community was suddenly destroyed, probably by the same Roman legion that besieged and took Masada, the desert stronghold that was occupied by Jewish Zealots, which is located just a few miles away. One large Qumran document was, in fact, found at the fortress of Masada, indicating that some of the Essenes may have joined the revolutionaries there and brought some of their manuscripts with them.[2]

The Dead Sea Scrolls include a complete copy of the book of Isaiah; a fragmented copy of Isaiah, which contains much of Isaiah 38–66; and references to every book in the Old Testament except Esther. The majority of the fragments are from Isaiah and the Pentateuch (Genesis, Exodus, Leviticus, Numbers, and Deuteronomy). The books of Samuel, in a tattered copy, were found and also two complete chapters of the book of Habakkuk. In addition, many nonbiblically based scrolls and fragments pertaining to the Qumran community were found.

Scholars unanimously agree that, based on paleography and archaeology, these materials, which were collected from eleven different caves in the area from 1947 to 1956, were written during the last centuries of the second temple—from ca. 200 B.C. to A.D. 100. Merrill F. Unger recognized the significance of the find, particularly the copy of Isaiah: "This complete document of Isaiah quite understandably created a sensation since it was the first major biblical manuscript of great antiquity ever to be recovered. Interest in it was especially keen since it antedates by more than a thousand years the oldest Hebrew texts preserved in the Massoretic tradition."[3]

The supreme value of these Qumran documents lies in their allowing biblical scholars to compare them with the Massoretic Hebrew texts of the tenth century A.D. Where comparisons were possible, if, upon examination, little or no textual changes are evident in those Massoretic texts, an assumption can be made that the Massoretic scribes had probably been just as faithful in their copying of the other biblical texts that cannot be compared with the Qumran material.

A comparison of the Qumran scroll of Isaiah with the Massoretic text revealed them to be virtually identical. Paul Little, in his book *Know Why You Believe*, remarks,

> A comparison of Isaiah 53 shows that only 17 letters differ from the Massoretic text. Ten of these are mere differences in spelling (like our "honor" and the English "honour") and produce no change in the meaning at all. Four more are very minor differences, such as the presence of a conjunction (and) which are stylistic rather than substantive. The final three letters are the Hebrew word for *light*. This word was added to the text by someone after *they shall see* in verse 11. Out of 166 words in this chapter, only this one word is really in question, and it does not at all change the meaning of the passage.[4]

R. Laird Harris, in his work *Can I Trust My Bible?*, observes, "This is typical of the whole manuscript."[5]

The Septuagint

The Greek translation of the Old Testament, called the Septuagint, also confirms the accuracy of the copyists who ultimately gave us the Massoretic text. The Septuagint is often referred to as the LXX because it was reputedly done by seventy Jewish scholars in Alexandria, Egypt, around 250 B.C. The LXX seems to be a rather literal translation from the Hebrew, and the manuscripts that we have are quite good copies of the original translation.

The Conclusion

In his book *Can I Trust My Bible?*, R. Laird Harris concluded, "We can now be sure that copyists worked with great care and accuracy on the Old Testament, even back to 225 B.C. . . . Indeed, it would be rash skepticism that would now deny that we have our Old Testament in a form very close to that used by Ezra when he taught the word of the Lord to those who had returned from the Babylonian captivity."[6]

The New Testament

The Greek Manuscript Evidence

More than three thousand different, ancient Greek manuscripts containing all or portions of the New Testament have survived to our time. These manuscripts are written on different materials. During the early Christian era, the writing material most commonly used was papyrus. This highly durable reed from the Nile Valley was glued together much like plywood and then allowed to dry in the sun. During the twentieth century many remains of documents (both biblical and nonbiblical) on papyrus were discovered, especially in the arid lands of North Africa and the Middle East.

Another material used was parchment. Made from the skin of sheep or goats, parchment was in wide use until the late Middle Ages, when paper began to replace it. Parchment was scarce and more expensive; hence, it was used almost exclusively for important documents. Such documents included the New Testament, of which some of the texts are extant.

Codex Vaticanus and Codex Siniaticus

Dating from the fourth century (A.D. 325–450), the *Codex Vaticanus* and the *Codex Siniaticus* are two excellent parchment copies of the entire New Testament.[7]

Oldest Papyrii

Earlier still fragments and papyrus copies of portions of the New Testament date from one hundred to two hundred years (A.D. 180–225) before *Vaticanus* and *Siniaticus.* The most outstanding are the *Chester Beatty* Papyrus ($\mathfrak{P}^{45}$, $\mathfrak{P}^{46}$, $\mathfrak{P}^{47}$) and the *Bodmer* Papyrus II, XIV, XV ($\mathfrak{P}^{66}$, $\mathfrak{P}^{75}$). From these manuscripts alone we can construct all of Luke, John, Romans, 1 and 2 Corinthians, Galatians, Ephesians, Philippians, Colossians, 1 and 2 Thessalonians, Hebrews, and portions of Matthew, Mark, Acts, and Revelation. Only the Pastoral Epistles (Titus; 1 and 2 Timothy), the General Epistles (James; 1 and 2 Peter; 1, 2, and 3 John), and Philemon are excluded.[8]

Oldest Extant Fragment

Perhaps the earliest extant piece of Scripture is a fragment of a papyrus codex containing John 18:31–33 and 37. Found in Egypt, the *Rylands* Papyrus ($\mathfrak{P}^{52}$) dates from A.D. 110–130. Critics had long asserted that the book of John could not have been written in the first century and, therefore, could not have been written by the apostle John.

Discovery of the *Rylands* Papyrus has forced the critics to abandon their position.[9] All of this early manuscript evidence creates a bridge of extant papyrus and parchment fragments—as well as copies of the New Testament—that stretches back to almost the end of the first century.

Versions (Translations)

In addition to the three thousand actual Greek manuscripts, more than one thousand copies and fragments of the New Testament survive in other languages—Syrian, Coptic, Ethiopian, Armenian, and Gothic—as well as eight thousand copies of the Latin Vulgate, some of which date back almost to Jerome's original translation in A.D. 384.

Church Fathers

A further witness to the reliability of New Testament text is found among the thousands of biblical quotations dispersed throughout the writings of the church fathers (the early Christian clergy [A.D. 100–450] who, beginning with Clement of Rome [A.D. 96], followed the apostles and gave leadership to the infant church). Someone has observed that if all of the New Testament manuscripts and versions mentioned herein (twelve thousand) were to disappear overnight, one could still reconstruct the entire New Testament, with the exception of fifteen to twenty verses, using quotations cited by the church fathers!

A Comparison

The evidence is conclusive for the early existence of the New Testament writings. The wealth of materials for the New Testament becomes even more significant when we compare it with other ancient documents that have been accepted without question.

Author and Work	Author's Life Span	Date of Events	Date of Writing*	Earliest Extant MS**	Lapse: Event to Writing	Lapse: Event to MS
Matthew, *Gospel*	ca. 0–70?	4 B.C.–A.D. 30	50–65/75	ca. 200	<50 years	<200 years
Mark, *Gospel*	ca. 15–90?	27–30	65/70	ca. 225	<50 years	<200 years
Luke, *Gospel*	ca. 10–80?	5 B.C.–A.D. 30	60/75	ca. 200	<50 years	<200 years
John, *Gospel*	ca. 10–100	27–30	90–110	ca. 130	<80 years	<100 years
Paul, *Letters*	ca. 0–65	30	50–65	ca. 200	20–30 years	<200 years
Josephus, *War*	ca. 37–100	200 B.C.–A.D. 70	ca. 80	ca. 950	10–300 years	900–1200 years
Josephus, *Antiquities*	ca. 37–100	200 B.C.–A.D. 65	ca. 95	ca. 1050	30–300 years	1000–1300 years
Tacitus, *Annals*	ca. 56–120	14–68	100–120	ca. 850	30–100 years	800–850 years
Seutonius, *Lives*	ca. 69–130	50 B.C.–A.D. 95	ca. 120	ca. 850	25–170 years	750–900 years
Pliny, *Letters*	ca. 60–115	97–112	110–112	ca. 850	0–3 years	725–750 years
Plutarch, *Lives*	ca. 50–120	500 B.C.–A.D. 70	ca. 100	ca. 950	30–600 years	850–1500 years
Herodotus, *History*	ca. 485–425 B.C.	546–478 B.C.	430–425 B.C.	ca. 900	50–125 years	1400–1450 years
Thucydides, *History*	ca. 460–400 B.C.	431–411 B.C.	410–400 B.C.	ca. 900	0–30 years	1300–1350 years
Xenophon, *Anabasis*	ca. 430–355 B.C.	401–399 B.C.	385–375 B.C.	ca. 1350	15–25 years	1750 years
Polybius, *History*	ca. 200–120 B.C.	220–168 B.C.	ca. 150 B.C.	ca. 950	20–70 years	1100–1150 years

*Where a slash occurs, the first date is conservative, and the second date is liberal.

**New Testament manuscripts are fragmentary. Earliest complete manuscript is from ca. 350; lapse of event to complete manuscript is about 325 years.

The Anvil Unharmed

In his book *The Bible and Archaeology,* Sir Frederic G. Kenyon, former director and principal librarian of the British Museum, stated about the New Testament, "The interval, then, between the dates of original composition and the earliest extant evidence becomes so small as to be in fact negligible, and the last foundation for any doubt that the Scriptures have come down to us substantially as they were written has now been removed. Both the authenticity and the general integrity of the books of the New Testament may be regarded as finally established."[10]

To be skeptical of the twenty-seven documents in the New Testament and to claim that their content is unreliable, one would also have to allow all of classical antiquity to slip into obscurity because no documents of the ancient period are as well attested to bibliographically as these in the New Testament.

B. F. Westcott and F. J. A. Hort, the creators of *The New Testament in Original Greek,* also commented, "If comparative trivialities such as changes of [word] order, the insertion or omission of the article with proper names, and the like are set aside, the works in our opinion still subject to doubt can hardly mount to more than *a thousandth part of the whole New Testament*"[11] (emphasis added). In other words, the small changes and variations in manuscripts change no major doctrine; they do not affect Christianity in the least. The message is the same with or without the variations. We have the Word of God.

The Anvil? God's Word

Last eve I passed beside a blacksmith's door
And heard the anvil ring the vesper chime:

Then looking in, I saw upon the floor
Old hammers, worn with beating years of time.
"How many anvils have you had," said I,
"To wear and batter all these hammers so?"
"Just one," said he, and then, with twinkling eye,
"The anvil wears the hammers out, you know."
And so, thought I, the anvil of God's word,
For ages skeptic blows have beat upon;
Yet though the noise of falling blows was heard,
The anvil is unharmed . . . the hammer's gone.

—Author Unknown

Is the Bible Inspired?

Rick Wade

Nonbelievers often ask, "Why should I believe the Bible? You have your Bible; Muslims have their Qur'an; different religions have their own holy books. What makes yours special?"

Such questions fall under the purview of apologetics, that is, they call for a defense. Our defense needs, however, theological and biblical grounding.

This chapter addresses the nature of Scripture. Is the Bible simply the remembrances of two religious groups? Does it consist of ideas conceived by mere humans—Jews and early Christians—as they sought to establish their religion? Or does the Bible consist of the words of God Himself?

Throughout history, the people of God have held the latter position. From the beginning, Christians have accepted both the Old and New Testaments as God's Word written. But two movements have undermined belief in inspiration. One such movement is the *higher critical* movement, which reduces Scripture to simply the recollections and ideas of a religious group. The more recent trend (although not organized enough to call it a movement) is *religious pluralism,* which holds that all religions—or at least the major ones—are equally valid, meaning that no religion is more worthy of belief than any others. If other religions are equally valid, then so are other holy books. Today, even some Christians are inclined to think this way.

Our evaluation of the Bible in contrast to other "holy books" is that the Bible is the inspired Word of God. If God's final word is found in the Bible, then no other book can be God's Word. To differ with what the Bible says is to differ with God Himself.

What does *inspiration* mean in a biblical context? Following the higher critics, many people—even within the church—have come to see the Bible as inspired in the same way that, say, an artist or a poet might be inspired. The artist sees the Grand Canyon and, her imagination flooded with images and ideas, hurries back to her canvas to paint a beautiful picture. A poet, upon viewing the devastation of war, pens lines of poetry that stir compassion in his readers. Is that what is meant when one says that the Bible is inspired?

Use of the word *inspiration* is based on 2 Timothy 3:16: "All Scripture is inspired by God and profitable for teaching, for reproof, for correction, for training in righteousness." *Inspired* is translated from the Greek word *theopnuestos,* which literally means "God-breathed." Some scholars translate *theopnuestos* as "ex-spired," or "breathed out." Inspiration, then, in the biblical sense, isn't the stirring of the imagination of the writer but is the means by which the writers wrote accurately what God wanted written.

This idea finds support in 2 Peter 1:20–21: "But know this first of all, that no prophecy of Scripture is a matter of one's own interpretation, for no prophecy was ever made by an act of human will, but men moved by the Holy Spirit spoke from God."

Before we proceed further, we should establish a working definition of *inspiration*. Theologian Carl F. H. Henry provides a good definition: "Inspiration is a supernatural influence upon the divinely chosen prophets and apostles whereby the Spirit of God assures the truth and trustworthiness of their oral and written proclamation."[1] Furthermore, says Henry, the writers were "divinely superintended by the Holy Spirit in the choice of words they used."[2] Although some things were "dictated" to the writers, for the most part, the Spirit simply superintended the writing so that the writer, using his own words, wrote what the Spirit wanted written.

The Historical View of the Church

In establishing any doctrine, the first place to look is, of course, the Bible. Before examining what Scripture claims for itself, however, it will be worthwhile to discover what has been throughout history the view of the church. Because of the objections of liberal scholars in regard to biblical inspiration, it would be informative to know whose position is in keeping with our predecessors in the faith.

At least until the nineteenth century, the church has consistently held to the inspiration of Scripture. One scholar has said that throughout the first eight centuries of the church, "Hardly is there a single point with regard to which there reigned . . . a greater or more cordial unanimity."[3] The great Princeton theologian B. B. Warfield said, "Christendom has always reposed upon the belief that the utterances of this book are properly oracles of God."[4] In the sixteenth century, the Reformers Martin Luther and

John Calvin were explicit in their recognition of the divine source and authority of Scripture.[5] B. B. Warfield, Charles Hodge, J. Gresham Machen, Carl Henry, J. I. Packer, and other reputable scholars and theologians over the last century and a half have argued for the inspiration of Scripture. And as Warfield notes, this belief underlies all the creeds of the church as well.[6]

The Witness of the Old Testament

Do the claims of the Bible itself, beginning with the Old Testament, align with the beliefs of the church?

The clear intent of the Old Testament writers was to convey God's message. Consider first that God was said to *speak* to the people: "God says" (Deut. 5:27); "Thus says the LORD" (Exod. 4:22); "I have put My words in your mouth" (Jer. 1:9); "The word of the LORD came to him" (Gen. 15:4; 1 Kings 17:8)—all these references to God's speaking demonstrate that He is interested in communicating verbally with us. The Old Testament explicitly states 3,808 times that it is conveying the express words of God.[7]

Furthermore, God was so interested in people's preserving and knowing His Word that at times He even told people to write down what He said: "Then the LORD said to Moses, 'Write this in a book as a memorial, and recite it to Joshua, that I will utterly blot out the memory of Amalek from under heaven'" (Exod. 17:14; see also 24:3–7; 34:27; Num. 33:2; Jer. 30:2; 36:2).

God spoke to people and instructed them to write down the words He said. Those writings have been handed down to us.

It should not be said, however, that *all* of the Old Testament—or the New Testament for that matter—was dictated to the writers. Most of the Bible was not, in fact, dictated. The point is that God is a communicating God, and He communicates verbally. That God is somehow unable or unwilling to communicate propositionally to man—a position that some scholars of this century continue to hold—is foreign to the Old Testament. God spoke; the people heard and understood.

What, then, does the New Testament say about inspiration? Consider the testimony of Jesus.

The Witness of Jesus

Clearly, Jesus acknowledged the Old Testament writings as being divine in nature. In John 10:34–36, "Jesus answered them, 'Is it not written in your Law, "I have said you are gods"? If he called them "gods," to whom the word of God came—and the *Scripture cannot be broken*— what about the one whom the Father set apart as his very own and sent into the world?'" (NIV, italics added). Jesus believed that Scripture was God's Word, which came to the prophets of old, and He stated that Scripture could not be broken. In Matthew 5:17–19, Jesus affirmed the Law as being fixed and above the whims of men.

Furthermore, Jesus drew on the teachings of the Old Testament in His encounter with Satan: "Man does not live by bread alone" (Deut. 8:3); "You shall fear only the LORD your God; and you shall worship Him" (6:13); "You shall not put the LORD your God to the test" (v. 16). All of these quotations are from Deuteronomy. Jesus prefaced each statement with *It is written* or *It is said,* and Jesus spoke only what the Father wanted him to speak (John 12:49). Thus, by quoting these passages as authoritative over Satan, Jesus was saying, in effect, that these were God's words. Jesus also honored the words of Moses (Mark 7:10),

Isaiah (v. 6), David (12:36), and Daniel (Matt. 24:15) as authoritative, that is, as carrying the weight of God's words.[8] Jesus also referred to Genesis, Exodus, Leviticus, Numbers, Deuteronomy, the Psalms, and five of the prophets.[9] He even referred to an Old Testament writing as God's Word when such an attribute was not noted in the Old Testament itself (Gen. 2:24; Matt. 19:4–5).

In considering the position of Jesus on the nature of Scripture, we also should look at His opinion of the New Testament. But the New Testament hadn't yet been written. How, then, can Jesus be cited as supporting the inspiration of the New Testament?

First, realize what Jesus was doing with His apostles. His small group of twelve was being trained to carry on the witness and work of Jesus after He was gone. Therefore, while often teaching the crowds in parables, Jesus taught the apostles with clarity (Mark 4:34). He sent them as the Father had sent Him (John 20:21) so they would be "witnesses of these things" (Luke 24:48). And because He promised to send the Spirit to help them after He left, both the Spirit and the apostles would be witnesses for Christ (John 15:26f.; see also Acts 5:32). The apostles would be empowered by the Spirit to bear witness (Acts. 1:4–5, 8), and the Spirit would give them the right things to say when brought to trial (Matt. 10:19f.). The Spirit also would remind them of what Jesus had said (John 14:26) and would give them new knowledge (16:12f.). John Wenham said, "The last two promises [reminding and giving new knowledge] . . . do not of course refer specifically or exclusively to the inspiration of a New Testament Canon, but they provide in principle all that is required for the formation of such a Canon, should that be God's purpose."[10]

Therefore, Jesus didn't identify a specific body of literature as the New Testament or state specifically that one would be written. He did, however, prepare the apostles as His special agents to hand down the truths that He taught, and He promised assistance in doing so. Given God's work in establishing the Old Testament and Jesus' references to the written Word in His own teaching, it is reasonable to infer that He had plans for His apostles to put in writing the message of the Good News, which He brought.

The Witness of the Apostles

Finally, what do the apostles tell us about the nature of Scripture? To understand their position, it is necessary not only to know what they said about Scripture but also to understand what it meant to be an apostle.

The office of apostle grew out of Jewish jurisprudence, wherein a *sjaliach* (one who is sent out) could appear in the name of another, bearing the authority of that other person. It was said that "the *sjaliach* for a person is as this person himself." As Christ's representatives, the apostles (*apostle* also means "sent out") carried forth the teaching that they had received. "This apostolic preaching is the foundation of the church, to which the church is bound (Matt. 16:18; Eph. 2:20)."[11] The apostles had been authorized by Jesus as special ambassadors to teach what He had taught them (see John 20:21). Their message was authoritative both when it was spoken and when it was written.

As the apostles were witnesses of the gospel, they also were bearers of tradition. In contrast to the contemporary understanding of tradition—a practice that derives from humans and may be changed—*tradition* in the Hebrew understanding meant "what has been handed down with authority."[12] Paul was referring to the latter understanding when he praised the Corinthians for holding to the traditions they had been taught and when he exhorted the Thessalonians to do the same (1 Cor. 11:2; 2 Thess. 2:15). The tradition of men, on the other hand, drew criticism from Jesus (Mark 7:8).

What Paul taught, he attributed directly to Christ (2 Cor. 13:3). He identified his gospel with the preaching of Jesus (Rom. 16:25). And he said that his words were taught by the Spirit (1 Cor. 2:13), writing to the Corinthians that his words were "the Lord's commandment" (1 Cor. 14:37). Furthermore, both Paul and John considered their writings important enough to exhort people to read them (Col. 4:16; 1 Thess. 5:27; John 20:31; Rev. 1:3). And Peter placed the apostolic message on a par with the writings of the Old Testament prophets (2 Peter 3:2).

To be an apostle, then, meant bearing witness of the gospel, maintaining divine tradition, and handing down—as Christ's authoritative representatives—the teachings of both Christ and the Holy Spirit.

Vested as they were with the authority of Christ, what did the apostles perceive to be the nature of Scripture? Many, if not most, Christians are familiar with 2 Timothy 3:16: "All Scripture is inspired by God and profitable for teaching, for reproof, for correction, for training in righteousness." This verse is often cited in support of the doctrine of the inspiration of Scripture. In this passage, Paul was speaking primarily of the Old Testament. For Paul, the idea of God "breathing out" or speaking wasn't new. Knowing the Old Testament well, he would have read that "the 'mouth' of God was regarded as the source from which the Divine message came."[13] Isaiah 45:23 says, "I have sworn by Myself, the word has gone forth from My mouth in righteousness and will not turn back" (see also 55:11). Paul would have also heard of Jesus' encounter with Satan in the desert, and would have recognized that Jesus quoted Deuteronomy when He replied to the tempter, "Man shall not live on bread alone, but on every word that proceeds out of the mouth of God" (Matt. 4:4; Deut. 8:3). Thus, Paul, recognizing the divinity of Jesus as well as the divine inspiration of Old Testament Scripture, attributed to the gospel teachings the same divine authority as that attributed to the Old Testament.

Peter also taught that the Scriptures were, in effect, the speech of God. In 2 Peter 1:21, he noted that prophecy was made by "men moved by the Holy Spirit [who] spoke from God." Peter recognized that prophesy did not originate within the minds of the prophets.

One further note: the Greek word *graphē* in the New Testament refers only to sacred Scriptures. *Graphē* was used in 1 Timothy 5:18 and 2 Peter 3:16 to refer to the writings of the apostles. Thus, both Paul and Peter ascribe inspiration to apostolic writing.

The apostles were the ambassadors of Christ, who spoke in His stead and delivered the message that was the standard for belief and practice. The message they preached was the one they wrote down. And the message was derived from their own recollections of what they witnessed and heard as well as from the empowerment of the Spirit. The New Testament, like the Old, claims to be the inspired Word of God.

Making a Defense

Concerning the inspiration of Scripture, it's one thing to establish the biblical teaching on the nature of the Bible itself; it's quite another to offer a defense to critics.

As was noted earlier, Christians frequently hear, "Many religions have their own holy books. Why should we believe the Bible is special?"

When this objection comes from a religious pluralist, the apologist will first have to question the pluralist on the reasonableness of pluralism itself. No evidence or arguments for the inspiration of the Bible will convince a person who believes that there is no true or false when it comes to religion.[14]

It's tempting for apologists to rely primarily on their arguments when responding to critics, which is something that even Paul wouldn't do (1 Cor. 2:3–5). What is learned from Scripture is the *power* of Scripture itself: "For the word of God is living and active and sharper than any two-edged sword" (Heb. 4:12). Isaiah 55:11 says that God's Word will accomplish His will. Acts 2:37 demonstrates the results of proclaiming the Word of God—people are changed.

What's the point? How many people who object to our insistence that our "Holy Book" is the only true Word of God have ever read any of it? Before launching into a lengthy apologetic for Scripture, we might invite the skeptic to read it and thereby give the Spirit the opportunity to open his or her mind to its truth (1 Cor. 2:6–16).

I'm not suggesting the abandonment of apologetics in favor of saying, "Look, just read the Bible and don't ask so many questions." The object is to move the conversation to more fruitful ground. Once a person learns what the Bible says, he or she can ask specific questions about its content, or we can ask what makes that person think that the Bible might *not* be God's Word.

The Bible clearly claims to be the authoritative Word of God and, as such, it makes demands on us. At the least, the tone of Scripture suggests that it is a book that has God as its source. But does the Bible give evidence that it *must* have God as its source? And does its self-witness find confirmation in our experience?

Regarding God's being the only possible source of the Bible, consider prophecy. Who but God could know what would happen hundreds of years in the future? What mere human—and even more unlikely, many humans over a period of hundreds of years—could correctly foretell more than three hundred prophecies about one person—Jesus?[15]

The Bible's insight into human nature and the solutions it provides to our fallen condition are also evidence of its divine source. Consider, too, that the Bible's honest portrayal of the weaknesses in even its heroes is evidence that Scripture has more than human authorship. The literature of a nation tends to build up its heroes while minimizing their failings. Not so, the Bible.

As further evidence that the Bible is God's Word, note its survival and influence throughout the last two millennia despite repeated attempts to destroy it.

What Scripture proclaims about itself finds confirmation, too, in our experience. The practical changes it effects in individuals and societies are evidence of its divine origin.

One more note. We have a further testimony from Jesus about Scripture: His resurrection is evidence that He knew what He was talking about!

The testimony of Scripture to its own nature finds confirmation through many avenues.[16] Regardless of the evidence, it is difficult to prove the inspiration of the Bible to anyone who isn't interested in reading it, to anyone who doesn't care to devote serious thought about it, or to the critic who wants only to argue. But we can share its message, make attempts at gentle persuasion, and answer questions as we wait for the Spirit to open the skeptic's mind and heart.

8

The Christian Canon

Don Closson

Nowhere does God itemize the sixty-six books that are to be included in the Bible. Many believers have at best a vague notion of how the church arrived at the canon of Scripture (*canon* meaning "measuring rod or rule"), and even after becoming educated, some believers are uncomfortable with the process by which the New Testament canon was determined. Many of them perceive it as a haphazard process that took far too long.

Furthermore, Christians—whether talking with a Jehovah's Witness, a liberal theologian, or a New Ager— are likely to encounter questions concerning the extent, adequacy, and accuracy of the Bible as God's revealed Word.

This chapter, therefore, considers the development of the Canon and considers, too, the changing perceptions of the doctrine of Scripture in the church age. Just how did the church decide on the books for inclusion in the New Testament? The discussion will include how the Canon was established and how theologians have viewed the Bible since the Canon was established.

The Early Church Fathers

The period immediately following the deaths of all of the apostles is known as the period of the church fathers. Many of the earliest church fathers actually walked with the apostles and were taught directly by them. Polycarp and Papias, for instance, are considered to have been disciples of the apostle John. Doctrinal authority during this period rested on two sources—the Old Testament and the notion of apostolic succession, that is, being able to trace a direct association to one of the apostles and thus to Christ. Although by the era of the church fathers the New Testament books had already been written, they were not yet universally viewed as a separate body of work equivalent to the Old Testament.

Six of the earliest church leaders commonly referred to are Barnabas, the writer of Hermas (unknown), Clement of Rome, Polycarp, Papias, and Ignatius.[1] Although these men lacked the technical sophistication of today's theologians, their writings and correspondence confirms the teachings of the apostles and provides a doctrinal link to the New Testament canon itself. During this early church period, Christianity was as yet a fairly small movement. These church fathers, often elders and bishops in the early church, were consumed by the practical aspects of Christian life among the new converts. Therefore, when Jehovah's Witnesses argue that the early church did not have a technical theology of the Trinity, they are basically right. There had been neither time nor necessity to focus on the subject. On the other hand, the early church fathers clearly believed that Jesus was God, as was the Holy Spirit, but they had yet to clarify in writing the problems that might occur when attempting to explain this doctrine.

The early church fathers had no doubt about the authority of the Old Testament, often prefacing their quotes with "For thus saith God" and other notations. As a result they tended to be rather moralistic and even legalistic on some issues. Because the New Testament canon was not yet settled, they respected and quoted from works that over time have passed out of the Christian tradition. The books of Hermas, Barnabas, Didache, and 1 and 2 Clement were all regarded highly.[2] Berkhof writes concerning these early church leaders, "For them Christianity was not in the first place a knowledge to be acquired, but the principle of a new obedience to God."[3]

Although these early church fathers might seem to have been rather ill-prepared to hand down all of the subtle implications of the Christian faith to the coming generations, they form a doctrinal link to the apostles—and thus to our Lord Jesus Christ—as well as to the growing commitment to the canon of Scripture that would become the New Testament. Clement of Rome said in the first century, "Look carefully into the Scriptures, which are the true utterances of the Holy Spirit."[4]

The Apologists

After the church fathers follows the era of the apologists and theologians, a period roughly including the second, third, and fourth centuries. During this time, the church took the initial steps toward establishing a "rule of faith," or the Canon.

Both internal and external forces caused the church to begin to systematize both its doctrines and its view of revelation. Much of the systemization came about as a defense against the heresies that challenged the faith of the apostles. Ebionitism humanized Jesus and rejected the

writings of Paul, resulting in a more Jewish than Christian faith. Gnosticism attempted to blend oriental the-
osophy, Hellenistic philosophy, and Christianity into a new
religion that perceived the physical creation as being evil
and Christ as being a celestial being with secret knowledge to teach us. It often portrayed the God of the Old
Testament as being inferior to the God of the New Testament. Marcion and his movement also separated the God
of the Old and New Testaments, accepting Paul and Luke
as the only writers who really understood the gospel of
Christ.[5] Montanus, responding to the Gnostics, eventually claimed that he and two others were new prophets,
offering the highest and most accurate revelation from
God. Although the Montanists were basically orthodox,
they exalted martyrdom and a legalistic asceticism that
led to their rejection by the church.

Although the term *canon* was not used in reference to
the New Testament texts until the fourth century—being dubbed so by Athanasius—earlier attempts were made
to list the acceptable books. The *Muratorian Canon* in approximately A.D. 180 listed all of the books of the Bible
except Hebrews, James, 1 and 2 Peter, and 1 John.[6]
Irenaeus, as bishop of Lyon, mentioned all of the books
except Philemon, James, 2 Peter, 2 and 3 John, Jude, and
Revelation. The *Syriac Version* of the Canon, which origi-
nated in the third century, leaves out Revelation.

Note that although these early church leaders differed
on which books should be included in the Canon, they
were quite sure that the books were inspired by God.
Irenaeus, in his work *Against Heresies,* argues that "the
Scriptures are indeed perfect, since they were spoken by
the Word of God [Christ] and His Spirit."[7] By the fourth
century, many books previously held in high regard be-

gan to disappear from use, were designated as apocryphal writings, and were seen as less than inspired.

During the fourth century, concentrated attempts were made both in the East and the West to establish the authoritative collection of the Canon. In 365, Athanasius of Alexandria listed the complete twenty-seven books of the New Testament that he regarded as the "only source of salvation and of the authentic teaching of the religion of the Gospel."[8] While Athanasius is prevalent in the Eastern Church, Jerome stands as his counterpart in the West. Jerome wrote a letter to Paulinus, bishop of Nola, in 394 listing just thirty-nine Old Testament books and our current twenty-seven New Testament books. In 382, Pope Damasus commissioned Jerome to work on a Latin text to standardize the Scripture. The resulting Vulgate was used throughout the Christian world. The Synods of Carthage in 397 and 418 both confirmed our current twenty-seven books of the New Testament.

The criteria used for determining the canonicity of the books included, generally, the internal witness of the Holy Spirit and, specifically, apostolic origin or sanction, usage by the church, intrinsic content, spiritual and moral effect, and the conviction of the early church.

The Medieval and Reformation Church

In the fourth century, Augustine voiced his belief in the verbal, plenary inspiration of the New Testament text, as did Justin Martyr in the second century. This view meant that every part of the Scriptures, down to the individual word, was chosen by God to be written by the human writers. But still, the issue of what should be included in the Canon was not settled entirely. Augustine included the Book of Wisdom as part of the Canon and held that the *Septuagint,* or Greek text of the Old Testament, *not* the Hebrew original, was inspired. The church fathers were sure that the Scriptures were inspired, but they were still not in total agreement as to which texts should be included.

As late as the seventh and eighth centuries some church leaders added to or subtracted from the list of texts. Gregory the Great added the books of Tobias and Wisdom and mentioned fifteen, not fourteen, Pauline epistles. John of Damascus, the first Christian theologian who attempted a complete systematic theology, rejected the Old Testament apocrypha but added the Apostolic Constitution and 1 and 2 Clement to the New Testament. One historian notes that "things were no further advanced at the end of the fourteenth century than they had been at the end of the fourth."[9] This same historian notes that, although we would be horrified at such a state today, the Catholicism of the day rested far more on ecclesiastical authority and tradition than on an authoritative Canon. Thus, Roman Catholicism did not find the issue to be critical.

The issue of canonical authority finally is addressed within the bigger battle between Roman Catholicism and the Protestant Reformation. In 1545, the Roman Catholic Church convened the Council of Trent in response to the Protestant "heresy." As usual, the Catholic position rested upon the authority of the church hierarchy itself. It proposed that all of the books found in Jerome's Vulgate were of equal canonical value (although Jerome himself separated the Apocrypha from the rest) and that the Vulgate would become the official text of the church. The council then established the Scriptures as equivalent to the authority of tradition.

The Reformers were also forced to face the issue of the

Canon. Instead of the authority of the church, however, Luther and the other Reformers focused on the internal witness of the Holy Spirit. Luther was troubled by four books: Hebrews, James, Jude, and Revelation. Although he placed them in a secondary position relative to the other books, he did not exclude them from the Canon. Calvin also argued for the witness of the Spirit.[10] In other words, it is God Himself, via the Holy Spirit, who assures the transmission of the text down through the ages, and not the efforts of any other particular group of people. Calvin rested the authority of the Scripture on the witness of the Spirit and the conscience of the godly. He wrote in his *Institutes*,

> Let this point therefore stand: that those whom the Holy Spirit has inwardly taught truly rest upon Scripture, and that Scripture is indeed self-authenticated; hence, it is not right to subject it to proof and reasoning. And the certainty it deserves with us, it attains by the testimony of the Spirit. For even if it wins reverence for itself by its own majesty, it seriously affects us only when it is sealed upon our hearts through the Spirit. Therefore, illumined by his power, we believe neither by our own nor by anyone else's judgment that Scripture is from God; but above human judgment we affirm with utter certainty (just as if we were gazing upon the majesty of God himself) that it has flowed to us from the very mouth of God by the ministry of men.[11]

He adds, "We ask not for proofs or probabilities on which to rest our judgment, but we subject our intellect and judgment to it as too transcendent for us to estimate."[12]

Modern Views

Although the early church, until the Reformation, was not yet united as to which books belonged in the Canon, they were certain that the books were inspired by God and contained the gospel message that He desired to communicate to a fallen world. After the Reformation, the books of the Canon were widely agreed upon, but now the question was whether they were inspired. Were they "God-breathed," as Paul declared in 2 Timothy 3:16?

What led to this new controversy? A great change began to occur in the way that learned men and women thought about the nature of the universe, God, and man's relationship to both. Thinking in the post-Reformation world began to shift from a Christian theistic worldview to a pantheistic or naturalistic worldview. As men such as Galileo and Francis Bacon laid the foundation for modern science, their successes led others to apply their empirical methodology to answering philosophical and theological questions.

Rene Descartes (1596–1650), although a believer, began his search for knowledge from a position of doubt, assuming only that he existed because he was able to ask the question. Although he ended up affirming God, he was able to do so only by assuming God's existence, not via rational discovery.[13] Others who followed Descartes built upon his system and came to different conclusions. Spinoza (1633–1677) arrived at pantheism, a belief that all is god, and Liebnitz (1646–1716) concluded that it is impossible to acquire religious knowledge from a study of history.

Thomas Hobbes (1588–1679) took another step away from the notion of revealed truth. He attempted to build a philosophy using only reason and sense perception; he rejected the idea that God might have imprinted the human mind with knowledge of Himself. Immanuel Kant took another big step (1724–1804). Attempting to protect Christian thinking from the attacks of science and reason, he separated knowledge of God, or spirit, and knowledge of the phenomenal world. The first type of knowledge was unknowable, Kant asserted, but the second type was knowable. Christianity was thus reduced to a set of morals, the source of which was unknowable by humanity.

The 1800s brought the fruit of Kant's separation of truth from theology. German theologians built upon Kant's foundation, which resulted in man's becoming the source of meaning and his relegation of God to obscurity. Frederick Schleiermacher (1768–1834) replaced revelation with religious feeling and salvation by grace with self-analysis. The Scriptures have authority over us, claimed Schleiermacher, only if we have a religious feeling about them first, and the faith that leads to this religious feeling may come from a source completely independent of the Scriptures.

David Strauss (1808–1874) broke completely from the earlier high view of Scripture. He affirmed a naturalistic worldview by denying the reality of a supernatural dimension. In his book *Leben Jesu* (*The Life of Jesus*), he completely denied any supernatural events traditionally associated with Jesus and His apostles, and called the resurrection of Christ "nothing other than a myth."[14] Strauss went on to claim that if Jesus had really spoken of Himself as the New Testament records, He must have been out of His mind. In the end, Strauss argued that the story we have of Christ is a fabrication constructed by the disciples, who added to the life of Christ whatever they needed to make Him the Messiah. Strauss's work would become the foundation for all since who question the accuracy and authenticity of the New Testament writers, and for the ongoing attempt, even today, to demythologize the text and find the so-called "real Jesus of history."

What Now?

As one reviews the unfolding story of how the canon of Christian Scriptures has been formed and then interpreted, a fairly accurate picture emerges of the changes that have taken place in the thinking of Western civilization. Two thousand years ago, men walked with Christ and experienced His deity first hand. God, through the Holy Spirit, led many of these men to compose an inspired account of their experiences that revealed to the following generations what God had done to save a fallen world. This text, along with the notion of apostolic succession, was accepted as authoritative by the emerging Christian population and would eventually come to dominate much of Western thought. In the sixteenth century, the Reformation rejected the authority of the Roman Catholic Church because of its claim to supersede the authority of Scripture. Later, the Enlightenment began the process of removing the possibility of revelation by elevating man's reason and limiting our knowledge to what science alone could acquire. This process gave birth to modernism, which is an attempt to answer all of the questions of life without God.

The wars and horrors of the twentieth century undermined and crushed many thinkers' trust and confidence in humankind's ability to implement a neutral, detached scientific mind to our problems and to determine truth. As a result, many people today have rejected modernism and the scientific mind. They have embraced postmodernism, a position that denies the ability to determine truth that is true for everyone everywhere. In fact, postmodernism claims that absolute truth does not exist. We can find personal truth only through individual experience. What does this mean for the theologian who has accepted the conclusions of postmodern thinking? One theologian writes, "At the present, however, there is no general agreement even as to what theology is, much less how to get on with the task of systematics. . . . We are, for the most part, uncertain even as to what the options are."[15]

This theologian argues that Christian theology can no longer rest upon metaphysics or history—neither an explanation of the nature of reality nor the historical record of any texts, including the Bible. We have the remarkable situation of theology divorced from any knowledge of God and His dealings with His creation. Not surprisingly, modern theologians feel free to integrate Hare Krishna, Zen Buddhism, and other traditions, with Christian thought—and especially Christian ethics. These eastern traditions, however, are not rooted in historical events and often deny any basis in rational thinking, even to the point of questioning the reality of the self.[16]

Once individuals refuse to accept the claim of inspiration that the Bible makes for itself, they are left with a set of ethics that has no foundation. History has shown that it rarely takes more than a generation for this kind of religion to lose its significance within a culture. How, then, do we know that Christianity is true? William Lane Craig makes an important point in his book *Reasonable Faith*. As believers, we know by the internal witness of the Holy Spirit that the Scriptures are inspired and that the gospel message is true.[17] We show to unbelievers that the gospel is true by demonstrating that it is systematically consistent.

We make belief possible by using both historical evidence and philosophical tools. Ultimately, however, the Holy Spirit is the One who softens hearts and calls men and women to believe in the God of the Bible.

The case for canonicity is the same as that for divine inspiration of the individual books of the Bible and their authors. God superintended not only the transmission and recording of the sacred texts but also the collection of those texts into the Canon. The critical question is whether the church formed the Canon or the Canon formed the church. The record clearly shows that early, general acceptance of the Canon occurred long before official councils addressed the issue.

9

The Old Testament and the Apocrypha

Don Closson

A fundamental issue that separates Roman Catholic and Protestant traditions concerns the Old Testament Apocrypha. Catholics argue that the Apocrypha was an integral part of the early church and should be included in the list of inspired Old Testament books. Protestants believe that the books of the Apocrypha are valuable for understanding the events and culture of the intertestamental period and for devotional reading but are not inspired nor should they be included in the Canon—the list of books included in the Bible. This disagreement about which books belong in the Bible points to other differences between Roman Catholic and Protestant beliefs about canonicity itself and the interplay between the authority of the Bible and the authority of tradition as expressed in the institutional church. Catholics contend that God established the church and that the church (i.e., the Roman Catholic Church) both gave us the Bible and verified its authenticity. Protestants believe that the Scriptures, the writings of the prophets and apostles, are the foundation upon which the church is built and are authenticated by the Holy Spirit, who has been, and is, active in church congregations and councils.

The books of the Apocrypha that the Roman Catholic Church considers to be canonical are first found in Christian-era copies of the Greek Septuagint, a translation of the Hebrew Old Testament. According to Old Testament authority F. F. Bruce, Hebrew scholars in Alexandria, Egypt, began translating the Hebrew Old Testament into Greek around 250 B.C. They did so because the Jews in that region had given up the Hebrew language for Greek.[1] The resulting translation is called the Septuagint (or LXX) because legend claims that seventy Hebrew scholars finished their work in seventy days. In Hebrew tradition, the number seventy held divine significance, thus the claims for the Septuagint's divine origins.

The books or writings from the Apocrypha that the Roman Catholic Church claims are inspired are Tobit, Judith, Wisdom of Solomon, Ecclesiasticus, Baruch, 1 and 2 Maccabees, Letter of Jeremiah, additions to Esther, Prayer of Azariah, Susanna (Dan. 13), and Bel and the Dragon (Dan. 14). The Roman Catholic Church does *not* consider three other Apocryphal books in the Septuagint, the Prayer of Manasseh and 1 and 2 Esdras, to be inspired or canonical.

This disagreement over the canonicity of the apocryphal books is significant if only for the size of the material being debated. Including the Apocrypha with the Old Testament adds 152,185 words to the King James Bible. Considering that the King James New Testament has 181,253 words, the inclusion of the apocryphal books in the Old Testament would greatly increase the influence of pre-Christian Jewish life and thought.

The issue of apocryphal material is also important for two other reasons. First, the apocryphal books support specific doctrines that the Roman Catholic Church holds. The selling of indulgences for forgiveness of sins and purgatory are two examples. Second, the issue of canonicity itself is reflected in the debate. Does the church, through the power of the Holy Spirit, recognize what is already canonical, or does the church make a text canonical by its declarations?

As believers who have called upon the saving work of Jesus Christ as our only hope for salvation, we all want to know what is from God and what is from man. What follows is a defense of the traditional Protestant position, which stands against the inclusion of the Apocrypha as part of the inspired Canon.

The Jewish Canon

In considering the debate over the canonicity of the Old Testament Apocrypha, or what has been called the "Septuagint plus," evidence shows that Alexandrian Jews accepted what has been called a "wider" Canon.

As was mentioned earlier, Jews in Alexandria, Egypt, began translating the Hebrew Old Testament into Greek (the Septuagint) approximately two hundred years before Christ. Because the earliest complete manuscripts that we have of this Greek translation of the Old Testament include extra books designated as the apocryphal books, many people believed that they should be considered part of the Old Testament canon, even though they are not found in the Hebrew Old Testament. Some people argue that we have, in effect, two Old Testament canons—the Hebrew canon, often called the Palestinian canon, consisting of twenty-two books (the Jews combined some Old Testament books, but the twenty-two books are identical to the thirty-nine Old Testament books in the Protestant Bible; see also note 7), and the larger Greek, or Alexandrian, canon, which includes the Apocrypha.

F. F. Bruce states that no evidence has been presented that the Jews (neither Hebrew nor Greek speaking) ever accepted a wider canon than the twenty-two books of the Hebrew Old Testament. He argues that when the Christian community took over the Greek Old Testament, they added the Apocrypha to it and "gave some measure of scriptural status to them also."[2]

Gleason Archer notes that other Jewish translations of the Old Testament did not include the apocryphal books. The *Targums,* the Aramaic translation of the Old Testament, did not include them; neither did the earliest versions of the *Syriac* translation, called the *Peshitta.* Only one of these Jewish translations, the Greek (Septuagint) and those translations later derived from it (the *Italia, Coptic, Ethiopic,* and later *Syriac*), contained the Apocrypha.[3]

Even the respected Greek Jewish scholar Philo of Alexandria never quotes from the Apocrypha. One would think that if the Greek Jews had accepted the additional books, they would have used them as part of the Canon. Josephus used the Septuagint and referred to 1 Esdras and 1 Maccabees. He states, however, that the Canon was closed in the time of Artaxerxes I, whose reign ended in 423 B.C.[4] It is also significant that Aquila's Greek version of the Old Testament, made about A.D. 128 and adopted by the Alexandrian Jews, did not include the Apocrypha.

Advocates of the Apocrypha argue that it does not matter if the Jews ever accepted the extra books because they rejected Jesus as well. They contend that the only important opinion is that of the early church. But even the Christian era copies of the Greek Septuagint differ in their selection of which apocryphal books to include. The three oldest complete copies of the Greek Old Testament that we have include different additional books. *Codex Vaticanus* (fourth century) omits 1 and 2 Maccabees, which is canonical according to the Roman Catholic Church, but also includes 1 Esdras, which the Roman Catholic Church rejects. Similarly, *Codex Siniaticus* (fourth century) leaves out Baruch, which Roman Catholics say is canonical, but includes 4 Maccabees, which they reject. *Codex Alexandrinus* (fifth century) includes three noncanonical apocryphal books, 1 Esdras and 3 and 4 Maccabees.[5] That certain books were included in these early Bibles whereas other books were not certainly indicates that inclusion alone does not prove their status as canonical.

Although some people might find unimportant the fact that the Jews rejected the inspiration and canonicity of the Apocrypha, Paul argues in Romans that the Jews have been entrusted with the "very words of God" (Rom. 3:2 NIV). And as shall be seen, the early church was not unanimous regarding the appropriate use of the Apocrypha. It would be illuminating to know, in fact, how Jesus and the apostles viewed the Apocrypha.

Jesus and the Apostles

Those who support the canonicity of the Apocrypha argue that both Jesus and His followers were familiar with the Greek Old Testament called the Septuagint. Supporters contend, too, that when the New Testament writers quoted Old Testament passages, they were quoting from the Greek Old Testament. Because the Septuagint included the additional books of the Apocrypha, Jesus and the apostles must have accepted the Apocrypha as inspired Scripture. In other words, the acceptance of the Septuagint indicates acceptance of the Apocrypha as well. Finally, supporters of this view contend that the New Testament is full of references to material found in the Apocrypha, further establishing its canonicity. But a number of objections to these arguments have been raised.

First, that the Septuagint of apostolic times included the Apocrypha is not certain. As was noted earlier, the earliest manuscripts that we have of the entire Septuagint are from the fourth century. If Jesus used the Septuagint, it might or might not have included the extra books. Remember, too, that although the fourth century copies do include the Apocryphal books, none includes the same list of books.

Second, F. F. Bruce argues that instead of using the Septuagint, which was probably available at the time, Jesus and His disciples actually used the Hebrew text during His ministry. Bruce writes, "When Jesus was about to read the second lesson in the Nazareth synagogue . . . it was most probably a Hebrew scroll that he received."[6] Only later, as the early church formed and the gospel was carried to the Greek-speaking world, did the Septuagint become the text often used by the growing church.

Bruce agrees that all of the writers of the New Testament used the Septuagint. None, however, gives us an exact list of what the canonical books are. Although it is possible that New Testament writers such as Paul allude to works in the Apocrypha, that fact alone does not give those works scriptural status. The problem for those who advocate a wider canon is that the New Testament writers allude to, or even quote, many works that no one claims to be inspired. Paul, for instance, might have been thinking of the book of Wisdom when he wrote the first few chapters of Romans. But what of the much clearer reference in Jude 14 to 1 Enoch 1:9, which no one claims to be inspired? A work called the *Assumption of Moses* seems to be referenced in Jude 9. Should this work also be part of the Canon? Paul also occasionally used Greek authors to make a point. In Acts 17, Paul quotes line five from Aratus's *Phaenomena,* and in 1 Corinthians he quotes from Menander's comedy, *Thais.* No one claims that these works are inspired.

Recognizing that the Septuagint was probably available to both Jesus and His disciples, it becomes even more remarkable that the New Testament contains no direct quotes from any of the apocryphal books that are being championed for canonicity. Jesus makes clear reference to all but four Old Testament books from the Hebrew canon, but He never directly refers to any of the apocryphal books.

The Church Fathers

Those who support the canonicity of the Apocrypha argue that the early church fathers accepted the books as Scripture. In reality, their support is anything but unanimous. Although many of the church fathers held the books in high esteem, they often refused to include them in their list of inspired books.

In the Eastern Church, the home of the Septuagint, one would expect to find among the early fathers unanimous support for the canonicity of the "Septuagint plus," the Greek Old Testament *and* the Apocrypha. Such, however, is not the case. Although the well-known Justin Martyr rejected the Hebrew Old Testament, accusing it of attempting to hide references to Christ, many others in the East accepted the Hebrew canon's shorter list of authoritative books. Melito, the bishop of Sardis, in A.D. 170 listed the Old Testament books in a letter to a friend. His list was identical to the Hebrew canon, except for Esther. Another manuscript, written by the Greek patriarch in Jerusalem about the same time as was Melito's, listed the twenty-four (see footnote for information on how the books were counted) books of the Hebrew Old Testament as the Canon.[7]

Origen, who is considered to be the greatest Bible scholar among the Greek fathers, limited the accepted Old Testament Scriptures to the twenty-four books of the Hebrew canon. Although he defends the use of such books as the History of Susanna, he rejects their canonicity. Both Athanasius and Gregory of Nazianzus limited the Old Testament canon to the books of the Hebrew tradition. Athanasius, the defender of the Trinitarian view at the Council of Nicea, wrote in his thirty-ninth festal letter (which announced the date of Easter in 367) of his concern about the introduction of "apocryphal" works into the list of Holy Scripture. Although he agreed that other books may "be read to those who are recent converts to our company and wish to be instructed in the word of true religion," his Old Testament agrees with the Hebrew canon. Gregory of Nazianzus is known for arranging the books of the Bible in verse form for memorization. He did not include the "Septuagint plus" books in his list. Eventually, in the 1600s, the Eastern Church did officially accept both that the Septuagint with its extra books was canonical and that the Septuagint is the divinely inspired version of the Old Testament.

In the Latin West, until the time of Jerome, Tertullian was typical of church leaders. He accepted the entire "Septuagint plus" as canonical, and was willing to open the list even wider. He wanted to include 1 Enoch because of its mention in Jude. He also argued for the divine nature of the *Sibylline Oracles* as a parallel revelation to the Bible.[8]

Jerome, however, was pivotal to development of the fi-

nal Canon. He was commissioned by the Roman Church
to create a Latin translation that the people could understand. The Vulgate translation was completed in 386. It
remains the official authoritative text for Roman Catholic
Bibles. Having mastered both Greek and eventually Hebrew, Jerome realized that the only satisfactory way to
translate the Old Testament was to abandon the Septuagint
and work from the original Hebrew. Eventually, he separated the apocryphal books from the rest of the Hebrew
Old Testament, saying, "Whatever falls outside these
[Hebrew texts] . . . are not in the canon."[9] He added that
the books may be read for edification but not for ecclesiastical dogmas.

Although Augustine included the "Septuagint plus"
books in his list of the Canon, he didn't know Hebrew.
Jerome later convinced him of the inspired nature of the
Hebrew Old Testament, but Augustine never abandoned
his support for the Apocrypha.

The Question of Canonicity

The relationship between the church and the Bible is
complex. The question of canonicity is often framed in an
either/or setting—either the Roman Catholic Church,
claiming for themselves absolute authority, decides the
issue, or we have chaos with no guidance whatsoever regarding the limits of what is inspired and what is not.

In the recent Rose Hill conference consisting of
Catholics, Protestants, and Eastern Orthodox theologians,
evangelical theologian Harold O. J. Brown asks that we
hold a dynamic view of this relationship between the
church and the Bible. He notes that Catholics have argued
"that the church—the Catholic Church—gave us the Bible
and that church authority authenticates it."[10] Protestants

have responded with the view that "Scripture creates the church, which is built on the foundation of the prophets and apostles."[11] Brown admits, however, that it is not possible to make the New Testament older than the church. Does this leave us, then, bowing to church authority only? Brown doesn't think so. He writes, "[I]t is the work of the Spirit that makes the Scripture divinely authoritative and preserves them from error. In addition the Holy Spirit was active in the early congregations and councils, enabling them to recognize the right Scriptures as God's Word." He adds that even though the completed Canon is younger than the church, it is not in captivity to the church. Instead, "it is the 'norm that norms' the church's teaching and life."[12]

Many Catholics argue that the additional books found in the Apocrypha (Septuagint plus), which they call the *deutero-canon,* were universally held by the early church to be canonical. This claim is, as argued earlier, a considerable overstatement. Protestants, however, have overreacted, as if these books never existed or played any role whatsoever in the early church. This position, too, is extreme. Although many of the early church fathers recognized a distinction between inspired Scripture and the apocryphal books, they universally held them in high regard. Protestants who are serious students of their faith cannot ignore this material if they hope to understand the early church or the thinking of its earliest theologians.

On the issue of canonicity, of the Old Testament or the New, Norman Geisler lists the principles that outline the Protestant perspective. Putting the issue in the form of a series of questions, he asks, "Was the book written by a spokesperson for God, who was confirmed by an act of God, who told the truth in the power of God, and was accepted by the people of God?"[13] If these questions, especially the first one, can be answered in the affirmative, the book was usually immediately recognized as inspired and included in the Canon. The Old Testament Apocrypha, however, lacks many of these characteristics. None of the books claim to have been written by a prophet, and Maccabees specifically denies being prophetic.[14] Others contain extensive factual errors.[15] Most importantly, many leaders in the early church—including Melito of Sardis, Origen, Athanasius, Gregory of Nazianzus, and Jerome—rejected the canonicity of the Apocrypha, although they retained high regard for its devotional and inspirational value.

A final irony in this matter is that Cardinal Cajetan, who opposed Luther at Augsburg in 1518, published in 1532 a *Commentary on All the Authentic Historical Books of the Old Testament.* The cardinal's commentary did *not* include the Apocrypha![16]

10

The Debate over the King James Bible

Rick Wade

Have you ever been in a Bible study in which two or three Bible versions were being used? Following the train of thought can be difficult when a verse in one version differs from the same verse in another version.

Since the 1940s, many new Bible versions have appeared on the market: the *Revised Standard Version,* the *New English Bible,* the *New American Standard Bible,* the *New International Version,* the *Living Bible,* the *Contemporary English Version, The Message,* and many more. When I was growing up in the 1950s and 1960s, the King James Version (KJV) was still the dominant version. Today, the *New International Version* leads sales, followed by the KJV.[1]

To some people, the multiplicity of versions seems confusing or needless, but they accept the fact that other people use other versions, believing that selection is a matter of personal preference. For others, however, the existence of multiple versions is a serious matter, not because of the inconvenience of multiple versions but because they believe that the KJV is the only correct version for the church.

The new versions came about because of the publication of a new Greek New Testament about a century ago.

Defenders of the primacy of the KJV were vocal in their opposition to the new Greek text and the new English versions that followed its publication. The debate over which version is most valid is not as heated today, but it remains a matter of concern for some Christians. Therefore, a discussion of the King James Version-versus-modern version debate is useful, focusing on the New Testament, for that is where the main concerns lie.

This debate is argued on two levels. On one level, the focus is on the KJV itself. Some people simply believe that this particular translation is the best. Proponents see a certain majesty in its language, and they appreciate its important role in the history of the church. The KJV has served the church well, say its proponents, and there is no need to confuse readers by publishing other versions.

The objections to the multiplicity of versions, however, go beyond style and tradition. Some Christians believe that newer translations of Scripture do not reliably convey God's truth. Some arguments for this position are little more than angry diatribes that are often circular. Some people say, for example, that because the new versions differ from the KJV, they are bad versions. The supremacy of the KJV is simply assumed.[2]

Although arguments from tradition and style can be powerful, other considerations might outweigh them. A significant problem with the KJV is, of course, the language. People who did not grow up using the KJV have a hard time understanding it. Some of its words are no longer in use, and the antiquated forms of these words as well as archaic syntax impede the understanding of the text. Over time, readers can learn to understand the style of writing, but without any more compelling reasons than tradition and style, many readers don't see why they should bother.

On a second level, this debate focuses on the Greek manuscripts from which the English versions are translated. Some KJV proponents believe that the Greek text underlying most of the newer versions is corrupt. As will be seen, the KJV proponents present some interesting arguments for their position.

Because the Greek text is central to this debate, this chapter—without getting too technical—focuses its examination upon the text. A brief history of the KJV will provide necessary background information.

A Brief History of the King James Version

An old joke goes, "If it was good enough for the apostle Paul, it is good enough for me!" Paul, of course, was fifteen and a half centuries too early for the KJV. The New Testament writers wrote in *koine* Greek, the language of the common man in the first century A.D. The first complete English Bible was not produced until John Wycliffe's translation in the fourteenth century. He translated from the Latin Vulgate, which was the most widely used version at that time.

The next major step in the development of the English Bible was Tyndale's translation of the New Testament, published in 1526, and portions of the Old Testament, published later. Tyndale's version was significant because it was translated from a newly published Greek New Testament rather than from the Vulgate.

After Tyndale's, a number of other versions were produced, among them were the Coverdale Bible, the Matthew Bible, the Great Bible, Geneva Bible, and the Bishops' Bible. In 1611, the KJV was published to provide a Bible that could be used by both Anglicans and Puritans. Marginal notes, reflecting any particular theological bias, were removed and the language used was that of the people.

As was noted earlier, Tyndale used a Greek text for his translation. The first published Greek New Testament appeared in 1516, and it was edited by Erasmus, a Dutch scholar. Erasmus had at his disposal no more than six Greek manuscripts (we have thousands of such manuscripts at our disposal today). These manuscripts were part of what is called the Byzantine text family.

Although Erasmus's edition proved a boon to the study of the New Testament, it had a number of problems. For one thing, none of his sources had the last six verses of the book of Revelation, so Erasmus translated them from the Latin Vulgate back into Greek. Thus, in his text "several words and phrases may be found that are attested in no Greek manuscript whatsoever."[3] In the first two editions of his New Testament, Erasmus left out 1 John 5:7 because it did not appear in any of his Greek manuscripts. That verse reads, "For there are three that bear record in heaven, the Father, the Word, and the Holy Ghost: and these three are one" (KJV). This omission created a furor, so he promised to include the verse in a later edition if it could be found in any Greek manuscript. One was brought forward and, although Erasmus did not think the text was genuine, he kept his promise and included the verse. The manuscript in question is now believed to have been a very late and unreliable one, and some scholars think that it was forged to include the verse in question.[4]

Erasmus's Greek text was reworked and reprinted by others, including Robert Estienne, who divided the text into verses. Theodore Beza then built upon Estienne's work, and his Greek text provided one of the major foundations for the KJV. The term *Textus Receptus,* or "Received

Text," came from a blurb in another Greek text produced in the early seventeenth century by the Elzevir brothers. This title is still used in connection with the KJV, and it is one you will see again in this chapter.

Westcott and Hort

As was noted earlier, the more substantial arguments of the KJV proponents focus on the Greek texts underlying the different versions. Four significant issues constitute the debate involving these texts: the science of textual criticism, the number of Greek manuscripts available, the history of the Greek texts, and the dates of the manuscripts.

Before examining these issues, it will be helpful to mention the historical event that brought the debate to a head and to introduce a central element in New Testament textual studies.

Comparing the thousands of Greek manuscripts available, scholars note many differences of one kind or another (although none affect doctrinal matters). Certain Greek manuscripts share enough similarities that they are believed to have come from the same source and are, therefore, grouped together. Each of these groups is called a *text family,* or a *text type.* Scholars generally agree upon four text families. The manuscripts that were used to produce the *Textus Receptus* (and later the KJV) were of the Byzantine family. The other three text families are the Alexandrian, the Caesarean, and the Western.[5]

The question of the most accurate Greek text family or families constitutes the fundamental debate between scholars in the King James Version-versus-modern version controversy. Which of the four families, if any, most accurately represents what the New Testament authors wrote? The Byzantine text was the dominant Greek text from about the eighth century until the end of the nineteenth century.[6] In 1881, however, two scholars named Westcott and Hort published a new Greek New Testament, which relied more on text families other than the Byzantine family. Their Greek text became the basis for the New Testament portion of most twentieth-century Bible translations.

Westcott and Hort evaluated the Greek manuscripts of the New Testament according to the principles of textual criticism—the science of the study of ancient texts, the originals of which are lost. Based upon their studies, Westcott and Hort argued that the Byzantine text was not the closest to the original writings, as the KJV advocates claimed. The Byzantine text seemed to have combined readings from other text families, and some readings seemed to have been modified for greater clarity and understanding. Thus, Westcott and Hort believed that the Byzantine text was at least two steps removed from the original writings. Also, they found no clear evidence of its existence in the writings of the early church fathers, and no copies exist from before the fourth century. Those who agree with Westcott and Hort believe that the Byzantine text was produced in the fourth century, probably in an attempt to give the church a single New Testament (a number of different Greek texts were being used at the time). Other text families, on the other hand, seem to have more original readings, are quoted by the early church fathers, and are thus considered to be closer to the originals. So the conclusions drawn from the application of textual criticism, along with the relative antiquity of the manuscripts, led Westcott and Hort to believe that the most accurate Greek text is to be found by drawing from all of the Greek text families, especially the Alexandrian family.[7]

Supporters of the Byzantine, or Received, Text responded that it was inappropriate to use naturalistic methods of study such as textual criticism on Scripture. They said that doing so amounts to elevating man over God in determining what the Bible says.[8] They also argued that the vast numbers of Byzantine manuscripts along with the centuries of history behind this text family should not be set aside on the basis of a few manuscripts discovered relatively recently. They insisted that the Spirit of God would not allow His true Word to lie dormant so long while the church was being guided by inferior texts.

Textual Criticism

As was noted earlier, those who argue for the Byzantine or Received Text say that it is improper to subject the Bible to the scrutiny of textual criticism. The Bible, being the inspired Word of God, is unique. One begins with it as inspired and then accepts what it says.

But those in the Westcott-Hort tradition note that we cannot simply shut our eyes to the fact that differences exist between the various Greek manuscripts, even those within the Byzantine family. Even those who believe in the inerrancy of Scripture recognize that only the original writings of the New Testament—not the copies—were inerrant. Our responsibility is to apply the most sound principles we know to determine what the original manuscripts said. This is the aim of textual criticism.

How does textual criticism work? Differences between Greek manuscripts are called *variants,* and they have several causes. Some variants are accidental, such as misspelled words or repeated or reversed words. Some variants resulted from a scribe's not hearing a dictation correctly. Also, deliberate changes seem to have been made to bring some passages in different Gospels into harmony or to make a doctrinal point clearer.

What sort of differences between the Greek texts show up in our English Bibles? One example is the Lord's Prayer as recorded in Matthew and Luke. In the KJV, the two versions are almost identical whereas in the NIV the prayer in Luke 11 is significantly shorter than that in Matthew 6. Most scholars believe that, at some point in history, a scribe added to the text in Luke to make it agree more with Matthew.

The last half of Mark 16 constitutes a lengthy section that is disputed. The KJV retains verses 9 through 20 whereas the NIV includes the passage with a note that says that those verses are not found in the most reliable early manuscripts. Scholars who believe that those verses should be excluded also note that the style and vocabulary are very different from the rest of Mark.[9]

To add one more variant, in the KJV, three verses in Mark 9 (44, 46, and 48) are identical: "Where their worm dieth not, and the fire is not quenched." The NIV puts verses 44 and 46 in footnotes and advises that some manuscripts include the phrase. Because each verse follows a reference to hell, it is very possible that a scribe simply repeated the warning to strengthen the message.

If all of this makes you nervous about the accuracy of your Bible, it is important to note that textual criticism is used on all documents for which the originals no longer exist. New Testament scholar J. Harold Greenlee noted, with respect to the Bible, "No Christian doctrine . . . hangs upon a debatable text."[10] This conflict provides no fodder for critics of Christianity who might ask how we can know what the Bible really says. We can be confident that we have a highly accurate text, especially given the number of New Testament manuscripts available and the antiquity of some of them.[11] As one writer has said, "It is well to remember that the main body of the text and its general sense are left untouched . . . textual criticism engages in turning a magnifying glass upon some of the details."[12]

Other Issues in the Debate

In addition to the question of using textual criticism, questions regarding the number of manuscripts, the historical dominance of the Byzantine text, and the dates of the manuscripts still should be considered.

Regarding the number of manuscripts, between 80 and 90 percent of existing manuscripts are of the Byzantine family and are in remarkable agreement. This fact is not in dispute. King James supporters say that the few manuscripts to which Westcott and Hort gave preference cannot override the witness of the vast majority of manuscripts in existence that are of the Byzantine tradition. Yet, one can argue that it is normal to expect that the oldest manuscript will have the most copies.[13] In response, those who follow Westcott and Hort point out that hundreds of copies could have been made from one defective text whereas a better text was not copied as often. The copying of New Testament texts, the argument continues, was not as carefully monitored as the copying of the Old Testament text by Jewish scholars. And, as has been demonstrated, errors were made and changes were deliberately introduced. Simply finding a lot of manuscripts that are in agreement is not enough to prove the reliability of that text. To illustrate their point, they ask whether one would rather have one authentic $100 bill or five counterfeits.

A second issue is the preservation of the text throughout history. Supporters of the Received Text ask why God's Spirit would allow the church to be under the authority of a defective text for almost fifteen hundred years.

Textual critics respond that this argument exaggerates the issue. They do not consider the Byzantine text to be a "'bad' or heretical text; it presents the same Christian message as the critical [or Westcott-Hort] text."[14] Again, no doctrinal differences exist between the Greek texts. Members of the Byzantine and other text families are used to determine what the true reading of a passage should be. The major text families are neither absolutely corrupt nor absolutely perfect. Text critics must use all available resources to determine what the original documents said.

Finally, the dates of the manuscripts are important in this debate. Textual critics point out that church fathers before the fourth century "unambiguously cited every text type *except* the Byzantine."[15] If the Byzantine text type comes directly from the original writings, one would expect unambiguous quotations of it from the beginnings of the early church. Textual critics also point out that no Byzantine manuscripts older than the fourth century exist, whereas copies of other text families older than that *do* exist.

In response to this assertion, KJV supporters note that the New Testament manuscripts began to be altered very soon after they were written. Eusebius, the ancient church historian, reported that heresies sprang up early after the turn of the second century, and proponents of these heresies sometimes altered Scripture to accord with their beliefs.[16] Thus, antiquity is not the crucial test. That no copies older than the fourth century exists likely results from the fact that the manuscripts were written on fragile material; one could reasonably conclude that the early copies probably wore out through frequent handling.

Come, Let Us Reason Together

Those who support the King James/Received Text tradition emphasize the number of manuscripts, the church's history with the Byzantine text, and God's interest in preserving His Word, whereas those who follow Westcott and Hort say that the variants in the manuscripts—even between those in the Byzantine family—prove the need for the textual criticism of the New Testament. The results of critical analysis, along with the ages of the manuscripts, lead those in the textual criticism camp to believe that the Byzantine family is just one text family that can lead us back to the originals—or close to them. It is not necessarily the one best text family upon which to base the entire New Testament.

Which side of this debate is more correct? If anyone is concerned about which Bible version is most accurate, that person should engage in more study on the topic. The texts cited in the notes for this chapter provide a place to start. It is, however, advisable to use a version that is as close to the Greek text as possible while being understandable. But whichever version a person chooses, one must be sure of his or her arguments before insisting that others use it, too. With all of the difficulties that we face in our often hostile culture, we should not erect walls between Christians on the basis of Bible versions. This is not to suggest that anyone take lightly God's Word. But more well-reasoned discussion is certainly to be desired, with the rule of love governing the debate.

Part 3

Jesus Christ

11

The Uniqueness of Jesus

Pat Zukeran

Jesus was either (1) an evil, lying villain; (2) a preposterously deluded madman; or (3) the Messiah, the Son of God. It is ludicrous for anyone who has studied His life and His claims to take the position that He was simply a good teacher. And only one of these three conclusions can be a true, logical possibility.

Liar, Lunatic, or Lord?

Jesus made outrageous claims that no ordinary or sane person would dare to make. First, He claimed to be God. He believed that He not only possessed the authority and attributes of God but also merited the adoration belonging to God. He proclaimed authority over creation, forgiveness of sins, and life and death. He stated that He was the source of truth and the only way to eternal life. Among the significant religious leaders of history, only Jesus ever made such claims.

What are some specific examples of Jesus' claims? When "Philip said, 'Lord, show us the Father . . .' Jesus answered: . . . 'Anyone who has seen me has seen the Father'" (John 14:8–9 NIV). Once, when the Pharisees were disparaging

Jesus and challenging Him, Jesus responded, "'I and the Father are one.' Again the Jews picked up stones to stone him, but Jesus said to them, 'I have shown you many great miracles from the Father. For which of these do you stone me?' 'We are not stoning you for any of these,' replied the Jews, 'but for blasphemy, because you, a mere man, claim to be God'" (John 10:30–33 NIV). In these two passages, Jesus claimed to be God, and His opponents understood His declaration of equality with God.

When Jewish scholars challenged His claim of authority over Abraham, the father of the Jews, Jesus replied, "'Your father Abraham rejoiced at the thought of seeing my day; he saw it and was glad.' 'You are not yet fifty years old,' the Jews said to him, 'and you have seen Abraham!' 'I tell you the truth,' Jesus answered, 'before Abraham was born, I am!'" (John 8:56–58 NIV). Jesus stated that He had existed two thousand years earlier and knew Abraham.

Regarding His power over life and death, Jesus stated, "I am the resurrection and the life. He who believes in me will live, even though he dies" (John 11:25 NIV). Thus, Jesus claimed authority over even life and death.

Finally, Jesus accepted worship and encouraged others to worship Him. Throughout the Gospels, and specifically in Matthew 14:33 and John 9:38, the disciples worshiped Jesus. Jesus states in John 5:22–23, "Moreover, the Father judges no one, but has entrusted all judgment to the Son, that all may honor the Son just as they honor the Father. He who does not honor the Son does not honor the Father, who sent him" (NIV). Jesus knew the Old Testament command "Worship the Lord your God, and serve him only" (Matt. 4:10 NIV). Despite this, Jesus encouraged others to worship Him as God incarnate.

How, then, after reading such claims, can anyone say that Jesus was merely a good teacher? A man making such claims must be either a liar, insane, or God Himself. The rest of this chapter examines which of these conclusions is most plausible.

A Villain, a Madman, or God Incarnate?

As was noted earlier, Jesus made some astounding claims about Himself. He presumed to be God, claimed the authority and attributes of God, and encouraged others to worship Him as God. If, however, Jesus was a liar, then He knew that His message was false but was willing to deceive thousands with His lies. That is, if Jesus knew that He was not God and He did not know the way to eternal life, He died and sent thousands of His followers to their deaths for a message that He knew was a lie. His deception would make Jesus history's greatest villain—and perhaps, a demon. He would have also been history's greatest fool because these claims were what led Him to His death.

Few, if any, people seriously hold to the position that Jesus was a liar. Even the skeptics unanimously agree that He was, at least, a great moral teacher. William Lecky, one of Britain's most respected historians and an opponent of Christianity, writes, "It was reserved for Christianity to present the world an ideal character which through all the changes of eighteen centuries has inspired the hearts of men with an impassioned love."[1]

To believe that Jesus was a great moral teacher would be inconsistent and illogical, however, if some of His teachings contained lies about Himself. He would have to be a stupendous hypocrite to teach others honesty and virtue while preaching the lie that He was God. It is inconceivable that such deceitful, selfish, and depraved acts could have issued from a being who maintained from the beginning to the end of His life the purest and noblest character known in history.

Since the "liar" conclusion is not logical, let us assume that Jesus really believed that He was God but was mistaken. If He truly believed that He had created the world, had seen Abraham two thousand years before, and had authority over death—and none of this was actually true—we can only conclude that He was deranged.

A study of the life of Jesus, however, does not indicate that He displayed any characteristics of insanity. The abnormality and imbalance we find in the mentally ill are not present in Jesus. His teachings, such as the Sermon on the Mount and other passages, remain the greatest and highest words on moral commentary ever recorded. Jesus was continually challenged by the Pharisees and lawyers—highly educated men whose modern-day equivalent would be our university professors. These Jewish leaders were fluent in several languages and known for their scholarship of the Old Testament and Jewish law. They challenged Jesus with some of the most profound questions of their day, but His quick and insightful answers amazed and silenced them. And, in the face of tremendous pressure and hostility, He exemplified the greatest composure. Thus, the "lunatic" argument is also unacceptable.

If lunacy and deception are not consistent with the facts, the third option must be seriously considered—Jesus *really was God.* The next question is, What evidence substantiates Jesus' claim to be God?

Messianic Prophecy

One of the most incredible areas of evidence is the testimony of prophecy. The Old Testament contains a number of messianic prophecies made centuries before Christ appeared on the earth. That He fulfilled each one stands as powerful testimony that He was no ordinary man. Using just eight prophecies illustrates this point.

1. Genesis 12:1–3 states that the Messiah would come from the seed of Abraham.
2. Genesis 49:10 states that He would be of the tribe of Judah.
3. Second Samuel 7:12 states that Messiah would be of the line of King David.
4. Micah 5:2 states that He would be born in the city of Bethlehem.
5. Daniel 9:25–26 states that He would die, or be "cut off," exactly 483 years after the declaration to reconstruct the temple in 444 B.C.
6. Isaiah 53 states that Messiah would die with thieves, and then be buried in a rich man's tomb.
7. Psalm 22:16 states that upon His death His hands and His feet would be pierced. This statement is quite significant because Roman crucifixion had not been invented at the time the psalmist was writing.
8. Isaiah 49:7 states that Messiah would be known and hated by the entire nation. Not many men become known by their entire nation, and even fewer are despised by the entire nation.

Consider the odds of someone's fulfilling all eight of these prophecies by pure coincidence. Suppose that there is one chance in a hundred that one man could fulfill just one of these prophecies. That means that when all eight prophecies are put together there is a one-tenth to the sixteenth power (0.1^{16}, or a decimal point followed by fifteen zeros and a one) probability that they were fulfilled by chance. Mathematician Peter Stoner estimates a one-tenth to the seventeenth power (0.1^{17}) that these eight prophecies were fulfilled by chance.[2] Mathematicians have estimated that the possibility of fulfilling sixteen prophecies by chance are about one-tenth to the forty-fifth power (0.1^{45}).[3] That's a decimal point followed by forty-four zeroes and a one! It is extremely improbable, then, that sixteen, or even eight, prophecies could have been fulfilled by coincidence by one man. Jesus fulfilled 109 major prophecies; the odds against His doing so by coincidence are staggering.[4]

Skeptics have objected to the testimony of prophecy, stating that the prophecies were written after the times of Jesus and, therefore, fulfill themselves. The evidence, however, overwhelmingly shows that these prophecies were written centuries before Christ. It is widely recognized, even by many liberal scholars, that the Old Testament canon was completed by 450 B.C. The Septuagint, the Greek translation of the Old Testament, which contains all of these prophecies, was completed in the reign of Ptolemy Philadelphus in 250 B.C. And the Dead Sea Scrolls, discovered in 1947, also contained copies or fragments of every Old Testament book, with the possible exception of Esther. Prophetic books such as the Isaiah Scroll were dated by paleographers to have been written by 100 B.C.[5] These prophecies for Messiah have thus been confirmed to have been written long before the birth of Jesus, and no religious leader has fulfilled even a minute fraction of the number of prophecies that Jesus has.

Confirmation of Miracles

Jesus demonstrated His authority over nature by walking on water (Matt. 14:25), multiplying bread (vv. 15–21), and calming the storm (Mark 4:35–41). He demonstrated authority over sickness by healing terminal and other diseases. His acts of healing did not require weeks or days; they were instantaneous. He healed blindness (John 9), paralysis (Mark 2), leprosy (Luke 17), and deafness (Mark 7). Such miracles cannot be attributed to psychosomatic healing but only to one who rules over creation. And as recorded in Luke 7 and Matthew 9, Jesus even displayed authority over death by raising the dead.

Some people question whether these miracles actually occurred, believing the miracle accounts to be fictitious legends that developed after the death of Christ. Philosopher David Hume argued that human nature tends to gossip and exaggerate the truth. Others argue that the miracle accounts were propagated in distant lands by the followers of Christ well after the events so that the miracle accounts could not be verified because of distance and time.

Several answers to these attacks can be presented. First, the Bible has proven to be a historically reliable document. Second, legends take a great deal of time to develop, usually well after the actual events, when they are impossible to verify by the testimony of live witnesses. The miracle accounts of Jesus, however, were being told in the very cities where they occurred and within the generation of people who lived during the lifetime of Jesus. Those eye witnesses to the miracles were still alive and included both followers of Christ and His enemies. These eye witnesses were questioned carefully by those in authority. If any claims were exaggerated or distorted, they could have easily been refuted. The New Testament miracle accounts would never have survived if the accounts had not been true.

German scholar Dr. Carsten Theide and British scholar Dr. Matthew D'Ancona in their book *Eyewitness to Jesus* conducted a scientific investigation of a fragment from the gospel of Matthew. Their findings revealed that the book was written before A.D. 70, possibly as early as the A.D. 30s.[6] If they are correct in their conclusion, the Gospels may well have been written and circulated during the lifetime of those who were best able to testify to the veracity of the miraculous events. What is clear, however, is that no one refuted Jesus' miracles.

Authority over Death

Perhaps Jesus' greatest demonstration of authority is revealed in His power over sin and death.

Many religions and religious leaders have claimed to know what lies beyond the grave. None, however, has demonstrated authority over the grave or confirmed his or her belief of what happens after death. Only Jesus has demonstrated such authority over death. All men have died, but Jesus is alive.

During His three-year ministry, Jesus exercised this authority over death by raising several people from the grave. The most notable account of His doing so involves Lazarus and is found in John 11. Here, even in the presence of His enemies, Jesus raised Lazarus from the dead. If this event were not a historical account, this story would not have survived. Its truth was verified and propagated in the very city where it occurred and within the lifetime of eyewitnesses—both followers and enemies of Christ. Those enemies of Christianity could at that time have easily refuted the account if it were not true. They could not, however, and they did not.

Regarding Jesus' own death and resurrection, the Old

Testament predicted the death of the Messiah in Psalm 22 and Isaiah 53. It also predicts, however, the Resurrection in Psalm 16:8–11 and refers to a future, eternal reign of the Messiah. The only way to reconcile these verses, which predict both a "death" and a "future reign," is the actuality of a resurrected Messiah.

Jesus Himself made such predictions regarding His own resurrection: "Destroy this temple, and in three days I will raise it up" (John 2:19). In Mark 8:31, Jesus taught "that the Son of Man must suffer many things . . . and be killed, and after three days rise again." In John 10:18, Jesus states, "I have authority to lay it [My life] down, and I have authority to take it up again." In each of these passages, Jesus predicts His own death and resurrection. Jesus was either mad to make such claims or He really had authority over death. His resurrection declares proof of the latter!

At the beginning of this study, we examined the claims of Christ, and they led to only three possible conclusions: Jesus was a liar, a lunatic, or the Lord. Because we showed the first two conclusions to be insupportable, our examination turned to Christ's claim of being God. His claims were confirmed by the record of prophecy, His miracles, and the Resurrection.

Human reason cannot explain how an uneducated man who was born in an insignificant part of the world, who taught for only three years, and then who died as a criminal turned the world upside down. He was unique among all men.

"One Solitary Life" is a famous commentary on the life of Jesus, written by an author who is said to be unknown. The final lines of that commentary provide a fitting conclusion to this chapter.

Nineteen centuries have come and gone, and today He is the central figure for much of the human race. All the armies that ever marched, and all the navies that ever sailed, and all the parliaments that ever sat, and all the kings that ever reigned, put together have not affected the life of man upon this earth as powerfully as this one solitary life.[7]

Additional Reading

Craig, William. *Apologetics: An Introduction.* Chicago: Moody, 1984.

Geisler, Norman L., and Ronald M. Brooks. *When Skeptics Ask: A Handbook on Christian Evidences.* Wheaton, Ill.: Victor Books, 1990.

Geisler, Norman, and William Nix. *A General Introduction to the Bible.* Chicago: Moody, 1986.

Hume, David. *An Enquiry Concerning Human Understanding.* Oxford: Clarendon Press, 1902.

LaHaye, Tim. *Jesus, Who Is He?* Sisters, Ore.: Multnomah Books, 1996.

Lecky, William. *History of European Morals from Augustus to Charlemagne.* New York: D. Appleton and Co., 1903.

Lewis, C. S. *Miracles.* New York: Macmillan, 1960.

Little, Paul. *Know Why You Believe.* Downers Grove, Ill.: InterVarsity, 1968.

McDowell, Josh. *Evidence that Demands a Verdict.* San Bernardino, Calif.: Here's Life Publishers, 1979.

Nash, Ronald. *Faith and Reason.* Grand Rapids: Zondervan, 1988.

Stott, John R. *Basic Christianity.* Downers Grove, Ill.: InterVarsity, 1971.

Theide, Peter Carsten, and Matthew D'Ancona. *Eyewitness to Jesus.* New York: Doubleday, 1996.

Walvoord, John. *Prophecy Knowledge Handbook.* Wheaton, Ill.: Victor Books, 1990.

12

The Deity of Christ

Don Closson

Some time ago, I received a letter in which the writer argued that there is only one God, who is called by many names and worshiped by people of different faiths. This kind of thinking about God is common today, but its wide acceptance does not reduce the intellectual problems that accompany it. Does this notion of God include, for instance, the god of the Aztecs who required human sacrifice? Or the warrior gods of Norse mythology: Odin, Thor, and Loki? And how does the Mormon belief that we can all become gods (if we join their denomination and conform to their system of good works) fit into the letter writer's theological framework? Even John Hick, an influential religious pluralist, believes that only some of the world's religions have a valid view of God. Islam, Christianity, Judaism, Buddhism, and Hinduism are valid, but Satanism and the religions of the Waco, Texas, variety are not. The belief that all religious systems worship one God raises difficulties in regard to the variety of ways in which different groups portray God and describe how humans must relate to Him.

The claim of one God for many faiths becomes even more of an issue when one religious tradition claims that

God took on flesh, became a man, and walked the earth. The Christian tradition has claimed for almost two thousand years that God did just that. The gospel of John proclaims that, "The Word became flesh and made his dwelling among us. We have seen his glory, the glory of the One and Only, who came from the Father, full of grace and truth" (1:14 NIV). John is, of course, talking about Jesus, and this claim presents an interesting challenge for every religious pluralist.

If what John and the rest of the New Testament writers claim about Jesus is true, then God in the flesh literally walked with and taught a small band of disciples. Furthermore, if Jesus was God incarnate as He walked the earth, we have a first-hand account in the biblical record of what God is like. Truth claims about God that counter those given in the Bible must then be discounted. In other words, if Jesus was God in the flesh during His time on earth, other religious texts or traditions are wrong when they teach about God or about knowing God in ways that contradict the biblical record.

The Deity of Christ

This chapter considers the evidence for the deity of Christ. Christianity's truth claims depend upon this central teaching and, once accepted, this claim reduces greatly the viability of religious pluralism, that is, treating all religious beliefs as equally true. For if God truly became flesh and spoke directly to His disciples about His own person and character and about such things as sin, redemption, a final judgment, false religions, and true worship, then the God of the universe expressed intolerance toward other religious claims—specifically claims that discount the reality of sin, that remove the need for redemption, and that deny a final judgment. Some people might not agree with God's religious intolerance, but then again, disagreeing with God is what the Bible calls sin.

Rather than begin with a response to attacks on Christ's deity by modern critics such as the Jesus Seminar or New Age gnostics, this discussion will begin with Jesus' own self-consciousness; in other words, what Jesus said and thought about Himself. Next, we will discuss the teachings of the apostles and the early church regarding the deity of Christ. The goal herein is to establish the fact that, from its inception, Christianity has taught and believed that Jesus was God in the flesh and claimed that this belief was based on the very words that Jesus spoke concerning Himself.

Christ's Self-Perception, Part 1

Jesus never defines His place in the Trinity by using theological terms. He did, however, make many statements about Himself that would be not only inappropriate but blasphemous if He were *not* God in the flesh. Remember, Jesus' life was not spent doing theology or thinking and writing about theological issues. Instead, His life was focused on relationships, first with His disciples and then with the Jewish people. The purpose of these relationships was to engender in them a belief in Him as their Savior or Messiah and their only source of salvation. Jesus told the Pharisees—the Jewish religious leaders of His day—that they would die in their sins if they did not believe His claims (John 8:24). And to one Pharisee—Nicodemus—Jesus said, "For God so loved the world that he gave his one and only Son, that whoever believes in him shall not perish but have eternal life" (John 3:16 NIV).

Millard Erickson, in his book *Christian Theology,* presents

convincing evidence that Jesus considered Himself equal
in essence with God.[1] Unless He was God, it would have
been highly inappropriate for Jesus to say, as He does in
Matthew 13:41, that both the angels and the kingdom
are His: "The Son of Man will send out *his* angels, and
they will weed out of *his* kingdom everything that causes
sin and all who do evil" (NIV, italics added). Elsewhere,
angels are called "the angels of God" (Luke 12:8–9; 15:10),
the phrase *kingdom of God* is found throughout the
Scriptures, and Jesus claims both authority over the angels
and the regency of the kingdom.

When friends of the paralytic in Mark 2:1–12 lowered
him through the roof, Jesus' first response was to say, "Your
sins are forgiven." The scribes knew the implications of
this statement; only God could forgive sin. Their remarks
demonstrate that they understood Jesus to be exercising a
divine privilege. If Jesus did not believe Himself to be
divine, He had here the opportunity to deny that He had
the authority to do what only God can do. Instead, His
response only reinforced His claim to divinity: "Why are
you thinking these things? Which is easier: to say to the
paralytic, 'Your sins are forgiven,' or to say, 'Get up, take
your mat and walk'?" (vv. 8–9 NIV). To confirm His authority to forgive sins, Jesus enabled the man to pick up
his pallet and go home.

Two other areas in which Jesus claimed authority were
the judging of sin and the observance of the Sabbath. The
Jews considered both acts to be God's prerogatives. In John
5:22–23 Jesus says, "The Father judges no one, but has
entrusted all judgment to the Son, that all may honor the
Son just as they honor the Father" (NIV). Jesus also claimed
authority to change humankind's relationship to the Sabbath. Honoring the Sabbath is one of the Ten Command-

ments, and the Jews had been given strict instructions on how to observe it. In the book of Numbers, God told Moses to stone to death a man who collected wood on the Sabbath. In Matthew 12:8, however, Jesus says, "The Son of Man is Lord of the Sabbath."

Clearly, then, Jesus made claims and performed miracles that reveal a self-awareness of His own divinity.

Christ's Self-Perception, Part 2

Comments that Jesus made about His relationship with the Father would be unusual if Jesus did *not* consider Himself equal in essence with God. In John 10:30, He says, "I and the Father are one." Later, in John 14:7–9, He adds that to see Him is to see the Father. Jesus also claims in John 8:58 to have existed before His incarnation on earth: "Truly, truly, I say to you, before Abraham was born, I am." Some people believe that the words that Jesus used here constitute His strongest claim to deity. According to the *Expositor's Bible Commentary,* this passage might more literally be translated, "Before Abraham came into being, I continuously existed."[2] The Jews recognized the phrase "I am" as one referring to God because God used it (1) to describe Himself when He commissioned Moses to demand the release of His people from Pharaoh (Exod. 3:14) and (2) to identify Himself in the theistic proclamations in the second half of Isaiah. Jesus also declares that His work is coterminous with the Father: "If anyone loves Me, he will keep My word; and My Father will love him, and We will come to him, and make Our abode with him" (John 14:23). The Jews who heard Jesus understood the nature of these claims. After His comment claiming to exist before Abraham lived, they immediately picked up stones, intending to kill Him for blasphemy.

In Jesus' trial, He explicitly declares His identity. The Jews argue before Pilate in John 19:7, "We have a law, and according to that law he must die, because he claimed to be the Son of God" (NIV). Matthew 26 records that at Jesus' trial the high priest tells Jesus, "I charge you under oath by the living God: Tell us if you are the Christ, the Son of God" (v. 63 NIV). Jesus replies, "Yes, it is as you say. . . . But I say to all of you: In the future you will see the Son of Man sitting at the right hand of the Mighty One and coming on the clouds of heaven" (v. 64 NIV).

This occasion presented yet another opportunity for Jesus to clarify any misconceptions concerning His relationship with the Father. Instead, He places Himself in a position of equality and of unique power and authority. Again, the Jews understand what Jesus is saying. The high priest proclaims, "He has spoken blasphemy! Why do we need any more witnesses? Look, now you have heard the blasphemy" (v. 65 NIV). The high priest calls for a vote of the council, and they demand Jesus' death (v. 66).

Further evidence of how Jesus perceived Himself is revealed in His use of Old Testament Scripture and in the way He made His own proclamations of truth. In a number of cases, Jesus began His statements with "You have heard that it was said, . . . but I tell you . . ." (Matt. 5:21–22, 27–28 NIV). Jesus gave His words the same authority as the Scripture. Even the prophets, when speaking for God, would begin their statements with "The word of the Lord came to me," but Jesus begins with "I say to you."

Other evidence of how Jesus saw Himself includes His claim in John 5:21 and 11:25 to have authority over life itself and His referring to Himself with the title *Son of God*, thereby indicating both His unique power and authority and His essential equality with God.

The Teaching of the Apostles

What did Jesus' followers say about Him? The gospel of John begins with a remarkable declaration of both Christ's deity and full humanity: "In the beginning was the Word, and the Word was with God, and the Word was God. He was with God in the beginning" (1:1–2 NIV). Later, in verse 14, John remarks that the Word became flesh and walked among human beings, and he identifies Jesus as the Word that became flesh. What did John mean by this remarkable passage?

The first phrase might be literally translated "When the beginning began, the Word was already there." In other words, the Word coexisted with God and predates time and creation. The second phrase, "The Word was with God," indicates the Word's having both equality with and an identity distinct from God. A more literal translation might be "face to face with God," implying the Word's having personality and coexisting in relationship with God.

Some groups, such as the Jehovah's Witnesses, perceive it as significant that the word *God* in the third phrase, "The Word was God," lacks an article. This, they argue, allows the noun *God* to be translated as an indefinite noun, perhaps referring to *a* god but not *the* Almighty God. The lack of an article for the noun actually makes a stronger case for the deity of the Word. In the Greek phrase *theos en ho logos,* the article *ho* before the word *logos* indicates that the sentence describes the nature of the Word; He is of the same nature and essence as the noun in the predicate; that is, the Word is divine. Interestingly, verses 6, 12, 13, and 18 of the same chapter refer unambiguously to God the Father and use an anarthrous noun, that is, a noun without the article.[3] Yet, the Jehovah's Witnesses do not dispute the meaning of these passages.

The author of Hebrews writes plainly of Christ's deity. The first chapter states, "The Son is the radiance of God's glory and the exact representation of his being, sustaining all things by his powerful word" (v. 3 NIV). The passage also states that Jesus is neither an angel nor a mere priest. In Colossians 1:15–17, Paul adds, "[Jesus] is the image of the invisible God, the firstborn over all creation. For by him all things were created: things in heaven and on earth, visible and invisible, whether thrones or powers or rulers or authorities; all things were created by him and for him. He is before all things, and in him all things hold together" (NIV).

Although Paul clearly attributes godlike qualities to Jesus, the use of the word *firstborn* often causes confusion. The word can be a reference to priority in time or supremacy in rank. Because Jesus is described as the Creator of all things, the notion of supremacy seems more appropriate. Philippians 2:5–11 also speaks of Jesus existing in the form of God. The Greek term used for *form* is *morphe,* denoting an outward manifestation of an inner essence.

Note also that New Testament writers used the word *Lord* for Jesus. The same Greek word that was used for *Lord* in the New Testament was used in the Septuagint—the Greek Old Testament—for the Hebrew words *Yahweh* and *Adonai,* two special names given to God the Father. The apostles meant to apply the highest sense of this term when referring to Jesus.

The Early Church

This examination of the claim for Christ's divinity has considered first Jesus' own self-concept and then what was determined by those who wrote the New Testament. It is not within the scope of this chapter to argue that the words attributed to Jesus by the writers of the New Testament are indeed His. Instead, it has been argued that the words attributed to Jesus do demonstrate that He claimed for Himself essential equality with God the Father. The traditional view of the Christian faith has been that God has revealed Himself as three separate persons—Father, Son, and Holy Spirit—who share a common essence.

Belief in Jesus' essential equality with God the Father was communicated by the apostles to the church fathers, who succeeded them in the task of leading the church. Although these early leaders often struggled with how to describe the nature of the Trinity with theological accuracy, they nonetheless knew that their faith was in a person who was both man and God.

Clement of Rome (ca. A.D. 96), for example, the earliest of the post-apostolic fathers of whom we have written record, addressed the church at Corinth, implying Jesus' equality with God the Father: "Have we not one God, and one Christ and one Spirit of grace poured upon us?" Later, in his second letter, Clement tells his readers to "think of Jesus as of God, as the judge of the living and dead." Clement also wrote of Jesus as the preexistent Son of God; in other words, Christ existed before He took on human flesh. Ignatius of Antioch spoke of Christ's nature in his letter to the Ephesians: "There is only one physician, of flesh and of spirit, generate and ingenerate, God in man, life in death, Son of Mary and Son of God."

Irenaeus of Lyons (ca. A.D. 140–202), answering the Gnostic heresy that Jesus was only a divine emanation, stressed the humanity of Christ: "There is therefore . . . one God the Father, and one Christ Jesus our Lord, who . . . gathered together all things in himself. But in every respect, too, he is man, the formation of God: and thus he took up man into himself, the invisible becoming visible, the incomprehensible being made comprehensible, the impassible becoming capable of suffering, and the Word being made man, thus summing up all things in himself" (*Against Heresies,* 3.16).

During the same period, Tertullian of Carthage (ca. A.D. 155–240) wrote of Christ's nature, that "what is born in the flesh is flesh and what is born in the Spirit is spirit. Flesh does not become spirit nor spirit flesh. Evidently they can [both] be in one [person]. Of these Jesus is composed, of flesh as man and of spirit as God" (*Against Praxeas,* 14). Later he added, "We see His double state, not intermixed but conjoined in one person, Jesus, God and man" (*Against Praxeas,* 27).

By 325 at the Council of Nicea, the church sought to systematize Christianity's response to various heretical views of Christ. The resulting Nicene Creed stated, "We believe in God the Father All-sovereign, maker of heaven and earth, of all things visible and invisible; and in one Lord Jesus Christ, the only-begotten Son of God, begotten of the Father before all the ages, Light of Light, true God of true God, begotten not created, of one substance with the Father, through whom all things came into being."[4]

The belief in Jesus Christ as being, in essence, God, began with Jesus Himself, who taught that belief to His apostles. They, in turn, handed down this belief to the church fathers and apologists. This chapter opened with the claim by some people that many different faiths worship the same God but merely call Him by different names. The deity of Christ is, however, the foundation upon which the Christian faith rests. What evidence is presented by those of other faiths to confirm that their religion is authentic, that their deity is indeed *the* deity? Christ's resurrection from the dead confirms His deity.

13

The Historical Christ

A Response to "From Jesus to Christ"

Rick Wade

C an we trust what the New Testament tells us about
Jesus? Or must we look elsewhere and possibly conclude that Jesus was just a man whose teachings became
the basis of a religion created largely by His followers?

For some fifteen years, New Testament scholars have
been involved in what has been dubbed the *Third Quest*
for the historical Jesus. The program "From Jesus to Christ:
The First Christians,"[1] which aired on the Public Broadcasting System in April 1998, brought this study to the
attention of the television audience. The program was intended to inform the public regarding the latest "new and
controversial historical evidence" about Jesus and the establishment of the church.

Those who hold the traditional view of the nature of
Christ and the New Testament were probably surprised
by some of the opinions presented in that program. The
narrator said that "archaeologists must sift clues, and scholars [must] decode the stories told by the first followers of
Jesus" to find the truth. He suggested that the differences

between Mark's and John's reports about Jesus' arrest are evidence that they aren't historically accurate accounts. One participant said that the gospel writers were giving only their own theology, using Jesus as a spokesman.

To the scholars featured on this program, Jesus was just a man who preached about the coming kingdom of God. He was not the incarnate Son of God. But He had enough charisma to attract a group of followers who liked His ideas and who sought to keep His memory and teachings alive after He died. With time, say these scholars, legends developed, and words and actions that weren't actually spoken or performed by Jesus were attributed to Him. The new Christians needed Jesus to speak to their own difficulties, so they put words in His mouth or invented miracles to address some particular difficulty that they faced.

The views aired on "From Jesus to Christ" are widespread among scholars, and they are the views typically heard on college campuses and in the media. Two assumptions made about the life of Jesus are accepted as common knowledge and typically aren't defended: *first,* that the Gospels aren't reliable historical documents; *second,* that no real supernatural element existed in Jesus' life and ministry. The belief that Jesus really didn't perform miracles or rise from the dead is, in fact, part of the reason that many scholars reject the Gospels as historical documents. One of the participants in the program, Professor Dominic Crosson, wrote in one of his books, "I do not think that anyone, anywhere, at any time brings dead people back to life."[2] Obviously, if one begins with an antisupernatural stance, one's treatment of historical accounts such as those in the New Testament will be affected.

The question of the historical reliability of the Gospels

is critical to Christians because Christianity itself rests upon historical events. If having true knowledge of these events is not possible, we have nothing upon which to base our beliefs. Without the historical events, Christianity becomes just another "belief system." In searching for the historical Jesus, which depends upon the historicity of the Gospels, some background information is first in order.

A Brief History of the Quest

The viewer of "From Jesus to Christ" might have thought that the program's title referred to Peter's statement in Acts 2:36: "Therefore let all the house of Israel know for certain that God has made Him both Lord and Christ—this Jesus whom you crucified." The scholars on "From Jesus to Christ," however, were not referring to the position to which Jesus was exalted by God the Father; they were referring rather to the position that Jesus' followers gave Him through the development of the Christian religion. In other words, His followers transformed Jesus, the man from Nazareth, to Jesus the Christ, the Son of God. The result, so claim the program's scholars, was an artificial bridge between the "real" Jesus of history and the Christ of faith. The scholars imply that much of what surrounds the man Jesus is mere mythology.

The preceding conclusion did not originate with any recent television program. In the last century and a half, three so-called quests have been initiated for the historical Jesus. The first quest began in the nineteenth century, when David Strauss published a book titled *The Life of Jesus.* Believing "that the Gospels could no longer be read straightforwardly as unvarnished historical records of what Jesus actually said and did,"[3] Strauss said that "unbiased historical research" needed to be performed to find out who Jesus really was. Why, though, did Strauss think that the gospel narratives could no longer be accepted at face value? As philosopher Stephen Evans says, "The quick answer is simply 'modernity.'" In the era of the Enlightenment, optimism about the power of human reason quickly led to the renunciation of the supernatural. Thus, reports of miracles and resurrections were now to be considered pre-scientific and mythological.[4] According to modernists, because so much of the Gospels deals with the supernatural, the documents were no longer to be trusted as historical.

In the 1940s, a second quest began with students of German theologian Rudolf Bultmann. According to Bultmann, very little could be known about the historical Jesus, not much more than that He lived and that He died on a cross. Some of his students embarked on a new effort to find the historical Jesus. This second quest continued until the early 1970s.[5]

In the early 1980s, the third quest for the historical Jesus began with the rise of a new enthusiasm about the prospects of historical study.[6] New archaeological and manuscript data have greatly increased our knowledge of Jesus' world. This third quest seeks to know who Jesus was by understanding the world in which He lived.

These three quests have been based upon the assumption that the Gospels are deficient in giving us a true picture of Jesus of Nazareth. It is tempting for orthodox Christians to dismiss these assumptions as liberal balderdash, but we should be careful not to throw out the baby with the bath water. Some revealing information is coming out of current studies.[7] Not everything, however, is to be accepted simply on the academic merits of participating scholars. The work of the Jesus Seminar—a splinter group that was represented in the program by at least three of the scholars—has drawn conclusions that even most liberal scholars reject. Rather, the arguments presented should be examined to determine if they hold water historically.

What follows, then, is a brief defense of the historical reliability of the Gospels.

Dating the Gospels

The assumption in "From Jesus to Christ" that the Gospels are not historically reliable records was very clear. Historian Paula Fredriksen said, "What [the Gospels] do is proclaim their individual author's interpretation of the Christian message through the device of using Jesus of Nazareth as a spokesperson for the evangelist's position" (FJTC, pt. 2). Because of the gospel writers' subjective interest, the program's scholars imply that the Gospel documents aren't to be taken literally as historically true. Scholars can cite at least three reasons for discounting the historical accuracy of the Gospels: (1) a late date for writing, (2) biased writers, and (3) differences between the Gospels. Consider first the question of dating.

Mainline New Testament scholars believe that the Synoptic Gospels—Matthew, Mark, and Luke—were written after the fall of Jerusalem to the Romans in A.D. 70. Mark was written first, drawing on earlier written and oral traditions. Matthew and Luke drew from Mark and still other traditions. Even conservative scholars recognize an interdependency within the Synoptics. The crucial issue here is *when* the documents were written. A late date would give more time for legends to develop and would suggest that they weren't really written by Matthew, Mark, and Luke.

Although the dates aren't firmly established, good arguments have been given for earlier dating, which would strengthen the case for the historicity of the Gospels. For example, Craig Blomberg, a professor of New Testament at Denver Seminary, provides several arguments for these early dates.

First, the early church fathers said that Matthew, Mark, and Luke were written by the biblical characters with which we're familiar. "No competing traditions assigning these books to any other authors have survived," he says, "if any ever existed."[8] In the late second century, for example, the church father Irenaeus said that Matthew composed his gospel before Paul was martyred under Nero in the A.D. 60s.[9] Second, Blomberg wonders why the early believers would have attributed these writings to such unlikely candidates as Matthew, Mark, and Luke if they were actually written by others. Mark and Luke weren't apostles. And Matthew, being a tax collector, didn't have an especially good reputation. Blomberg says that, in contrast, "the apocryphal Gospels consistently picked more well-known and exemplary figures for their fictitious authors—for example, Philip, Peter, James, Bartholomew or Mary."[10]

A third argument that Blomberg presents is built upon the date of the book of Acts. Acts ends abruptly with no record of what happened to Paul, although it does mention the martyrdom of Stephen and James. Why would Luke have left out such important information if he wrote the book a decade or more after Paul's death? And why would he make no mention of the fall of Jerusalem in A.D. 70? The likely explanation for the abrupt ending of Acts is that it was written as the events unfolded, in other words, while Paul was still alive (Paul died in the mid-60s). If so, then Luke's gospel—as the first part of his two-part history—must have been written even earlier. Because Luke drew from Mark, Mark must have been written earlier still.

A case can be made, then, that the Synoptic Gospels were written within perhaps thirty to thirty-five years of Jesus death. If they were written soon after the actual events, errors or misinformation would have been detected and either exposed or corrected.[11]

The Gospel Writers and Historical Truth

Assuming early dates for the Synoptics still leaves unanswered whether the writers *intended* to write factual history.

On "From Jesus to Christ," Professor Crosson suggested that we are mistaken in taking the Gospels factually because the writers didn't intend us to do so. He says that the issue "is whether the people who told us the stories in the ancient world took them all literally, and now we're so smart that we know to take them symbolically, or they all intended them symbolically and we're so dumb that we've been taking them literally" (FJTC, pt. 2). Crosson chooses the second option. He says, "I think we have been misinterpreting these stories because the people who write [*sic*] them don't seem the least bit worried about their diversity. We see the problem and then we want to insist that they're literal. I think that we have misread the Scriptures, not that they have miswritten them" (FJTC, pt. 2).

Certain scholars suggest that Matthew inflated the importance of the Pharisees in his gospel because they were so influential later in the first century when the book was written. Mark, they say, presented Jesus as the victim of persecution because Mark's community was likewise suffering. And Luke embellished his narrative with "shipwrecks and exotic animals and exotic vegetation" to make it more in keeping with the novelistic literature of his time (FJTC, pt. 2).

It's true that each writer chose events, conversations, and teachings that he thought were significant and would be meaningful to his audience. This doesn't mean, however, that the writers made up the stories.

In support of the veracity of the Gospels, Craig Blomberg points to the opening statement in Luke's gospel: "I [Luke] have carefully investigated everything from the beginning . . . to write an orderly account" (Luke 1:3 NIV).[12] Luke wanted to record the truth.

But were Luke's sources themselves concerned with accurately passing on what Jesus said and did? Some people believe that, because the church thought Jesus was returning soon, the witnesses wouldn't have worried about accurate reporting. However, it isn't certain that Jesus' followers thought that His return was imminent. Further the Jewish writers came from a long tradition for accurate record keeping. The Israelites had kept accurate records of the statements that the prophets had made, even though the Day of the Lord was expected at any time (Joel 2:1; Obad. 15; Hab. 2:3). Accuracy in handling the words of Jesus, who was considered to be greater than a prophet, would have been very important to early believers.

Blomberg notes, too, that if the gospel writers had devised the words and works of Jesus to suit the needs of the early church, one might expect that they would have addressed controversies that arose after Jesus ascended to heaven. The writers could have put in Jesus' mouth answers to controversial matters such as circumcision, whether Christians could divorce non-Christian spouses, and speaking in tongues. It seems, however, that "the first

Christians *were* interested in preserving the distinction between what happened during Jesus' life and what was debated later in the churches."

In regard to the accuracy of the Gospels, then, it is not, as Prof. Crosson claims, "dumb" to believe that the gospel writers intended to give us factual history.

Differences Among the Gospels

A crucial piece of evidence to support the view of scholars on "From Jesus to Christ" involves disparities between the gospel writers' reports. The sequence of some events and some of the things that Jesus said are recorded somewhat differently from one gospel to the next, indicating that the Gospels aren't accurate historical documents.

Dominic Crosson gives as an example the accounts in Mark and John of the night before Jesus' death. Mark has Jesus in agony over His coming death whereas John shows a more victorious Jesus standing up against the troops that came to arrest Him. Crosson concludes, "You have a Jesus out of control, almost, in Mark; a Jesus totally in control in John. . . . Neither of them are [*sic*] historical," he says. "I don't think either of them know [*sic*] exactly what happened" (FJTC, pt. 2).

Professor Crosson overlooks a common phenomena that occurs when any two witnesses testify to factual events—both writers told the truth, but each told only *his part* of the truth. The events recorded in the four Gospels can, however, be put together to form a coherent account of what happened in the Garden of Gethsemane.[13] Blomberg argues that the gospel writers were capable of remembering what Jesus said and did, but they weren't concerned about recording every element of each event or noting Jesus' every statement word for word.

Note that the written word was rare in the ancient world; oral transmission was the primary means of passing on knowledge. Therefore, people learned to memorize a great deal of information. Rote memorization, notes Blomberg, was the method of education for Jewish boys, and rabbis were encouraged to memorize the entire Old Testament.[14]

Yet, as conservative New Testament scholar Darrell Bock points out, the tradition for reporting history in the Greco-Roman world involved a "concern for accuracy in reporting the gist of what had been said, even if the exact words were not remembered or recorded."[15] Ancient historians didn't take it upon themselves to make up speeches and put them in others' mouths. They saw it as their duty to record what actually transpired and to report what was said. Adds Blomberg, certain details could be omitted and the sequence of events could be changed *"so long as the major events of the narratives and their significance were not altered"* (italics his).[16]

This fact shouldn't alarm those of us who accept the Gospels as God's inspired Word. In our own experience, for example, we don't question the word of an attentive and trustworthy person who summarizes a speech that he or she has heard. Or suppose that I said, "The Mind Games director asked me today to participate in an up-coming conference." I'd be telling you the truth about what the director said even if I didn't quote him verbatim. We can't deny that Jesus' words and deeds are reported somewhat differently from Gospel to Gospel. Understanding the method of ancient historians, however, assures us that we have been given the truth about Jesus. Paul's testimony that "all Scripture is inspired by God" (2 Tim. 3:16) assures us that the Gospel writers gave us the truth exactly as God wanted it presented.

This chapter has shown the probability of the Gospels' being historical truth because they were written soon enough after the events to insure against the creation of legend, that the gospel writers *intended* to report what really happened, and that the differences between the Gospels do not constitute a valid case against their being actual history. There is no reason, then, short of theological bias, to reject what is in the Gospels, and instead search elsewhere for the historical Jesus.

When the participants of the Jesus Seminar had completed their work, the historical Jesus was reduced to a simple peasant who was later revered and deified. This portrayal simply cannot explain the explosion of Christianity in the first and second centuries. If Jesus was, as the seminar implies, little more than the "Christian dummy" of the first century church, the community emerges as more brilliant than the leader! Even Renan, the French skeptic said, "It would take a Jesus to forge a Jesus." No, the Jesus of the New Testament—not the simple peasant of the Jesus Seminar—is the more likely candidate to be the center of Christianity.

The scholars who were involved in the program "From Jesus to Christ" have benefited the church by their archeological finds and new information about the world in which Jesus lived. They have erred, however, in rejecting the clear message of Jesus in the Gospels. The Christ of faith *is* the Jesus of history.

14

The Resurrection: Fact or Fiction?

Pat Zukeran

The most significant event in history is the resurrection of Jesus Christ. It is the strongest evidence that Jesus is the Son of God. And when His critics asked for some sign to prove His authoritative claims, He said, "An evil and adulterous generation craves for a sign; and yet no sign shall be given to it but the sign of Jonah the prophet; for just as Jonah was three days and three nights in the belly of the sea monster, so shall the Son of Man be three days and three nights in the heart of the earth" (Matt. 12:39–40).

The Resurrection gives men and women the sure hope of eternal life; it is an event that not only gives us joy as we look to the future but also provides powerful reasons to live today. Throughout the centuries, however, scholars and skeptics have denied that the Resurrection actually occurred. Our schools teach with history books that cannot abide the supernatural and that give alternative explanations for what occurred on that Sunday morning long ago. In some cases, the books fail even to mention that unique event, choosing rather to omit it.

This chapter examines the evidence for the Resurrection and determines whether this event is historical fact or merely fiction. First, however, we must establish that Jesus Christ was a true historical person and not merely a legend. A number of ancient source documents attest to the historical life of Jesus. First are the four Gospels themselves. Matthew, Mark, Luke, and John recorded numerous and specific details about the events surrounding the life of Jesus, and archaeology has generally acknowledged the historical accuracy of the New Testament. Hundreds of facts—such as the names of officials, geographic sites, financial currencies, and the dates of events—have been confirmed. Sir William Ramsay, one of the greatest geographers of the nineteenth century, became convinced of the accuracy of the New Testament as a result of the evidence he discovered during his research. His findings completely reversed his antagonism toward Christianity.

Textual evidence shows that the Gospels were written and circulated during the lifetime of those who witnessed the events. And, because so many specific names and places were mentioned, eyewitnesses could have easily discredited these writings if they had been false. The New Testament never would have survived had its facts been inaccurate. And the facts confirm that the Gospels are historically reliable, including the assertion that Jesus was a historical figure.

Another document that supports the historicity of Jesus is the work of Josephus, a Jewish historian (A.D. 37–100), a source that one might expect to be hostile toward proving the existence of Jesus. In his work *Antiquities of the Jews 3.3,* Josephus wrote, "Now there was about that time Jesus, a wise man, if it be lawful to call him a man."[1] Josephus relates other specific details about Jesus' life and death that corroborate the testimony of the four Gospel writers. Three Roman historians—Suetonius (A.D. 70–121), Tacitus (A.D. 55–120), and Pliny the Younger (A.D. 51–114)—also refer to Jesus in their writings, confirming Him as a genuine, historical individual.

Given the actual existence of Jesus, skeptics nonetheless challenge Christians to prove scientifically the Resurrection. The scientific method, however, is based upon demonstrating proofs through observation of the repeated behaviors or events. Therefore, the scientific method is limited to repeatable events or observable objects. Historical events cannot be repeated. We cannot observe, for example, a repeated creation of our solar system, but that does not mean that the creation of the solar system did not occur.

Thus far, we have shown that belief in the historical Jesus of the New Testament is certainly reasonable. Given the existence of Jesus, then, proving the historical event of the Resurrection depends upon an examination of the historical evidence.

Examining the Evidence

When investigating the Resurrection, one must reckon with the following three pieces of evidences: (1) the empty tomb, (2) the transformation of the apostles, and (3) the preaching of the Resurrection, which was first proclaimed in Jerusalem.

Consider first the empty tomb. Jesus was a well-known figure in Israel, and His burial site was familiar to many people. In fact, Matthew records the exact location: "And Joseph took the body and wrapped it in a clean linen cloth, and laid it in his own new tomb" (Matt. 27:59–60). Mark asserts that Joseph was "a prominent member of the Council" (Mark 15:43). If the tomb had not been found empty, it would have been destructive to the writers' claim to invent a man of such prominence, name him specifically, and designate the tomb site because eyewitnesses would have easily discredited the author's fallacious claims.

Both Jewish and Roman sources testify to an empty tomb. Matthew 28:12–13 states that the chief priests invented the story that the disciples stole the body. This fabrication would have been unnecessary if the tomb had not been empty. And later, when the Jewish authorities were eager to put an end to Christianity and the preaching of the apostles, they needed only to produce the body of Jesus, but they did not do so because there was no body to produce. The tomb was empty.

Furthermore, the corpse of Jesus was never found. Not one historical record from the first or second century attacks the factuality of the empty tomb or claims discovery of the corpse. Tom Anderson, former president of the California Trial Lawyers Association, states,

> Let's assume that the written accounts of His appearances to hundreds of people are false. I want to pose a question. With an event so well publicized, don't you think that it's reasonable that one historian, one eye witness, one antagonist would record for all time that he had seen Christ's body? . . . The silence of history is deafening when it comes to the testimony against the resurrection.[2]

The second evidence to be explained is the sudden, dramatic change in the lives of the apostles. The Gospels record that while Jesus was on trial, His disciples deserted Him in fear. Yet, ten of the eleven apostles (minus Judas) died as martyrs, proclaiming that Christ rose from the dead. What could account for their transformation from deserters into men who were willing to die rather than deny the validity of such a story? It would take a most compelling reason to account for such remarkable behavior by these men.

Third, the apostles began the proclamation of the Resurrection in Jerusalem, the very city where Jesus was crucified. Jerusalem was the most hostile city in which to preach because all of the evidence and witnesses in support of the event were present for everyone to investigate or interrogate. Legends ordinarily take root in foreign lands or develop centuries after the event, thereby making such legends difficult to discredit because the facts are hard to verify. In this case, however, the preaching begins in the very city where the event took place, and the preaching began immediately after the event occurred. Every possible fact could have been investigated thoroughly.

Five Common Explanations

Before critics dismiss the Resurrection, they must address the preceding evidence. And over the years, five different arguments have been waged against the truth of the Resurrection.

The Wrong-Tomb Theory

Critics of the Resurrection state that, according to the gospel accounts, the women visited the grave early in the morning while it was dark. As a result of the darkness and their emotional condition, they visited the wrong tomb. Overjoyed to see that it was empty, they rushed back to tell the disciples that Jesus had risen. The disciples, in turn, ran into Jerusalem to proclaim the Resurrection.

One can cite several flaws in this argument. First, it is

doubtful that the apostles would not have corrected the women's error. The gospel of John gives, in fact, a detailed account of their attempting to do just that. Second, the tomb site was known by not only the followers of Christ but also their opponents. The Gospels relate that the body was buried in the tomb of Joseph of Arimathea, a member of the Jewish council. If the body still remained in the tomb while the apostles began preaching, the authorities simply would have gone to the correct tomb, produced the body, and paraded it through the streets. This action would have ended the Christian faith once and for all. Remember, the preaching of the Resurrection began in Jerusalem, and the crucifixion site and the tomb were mere steps away, outside the city wall. The wrong-tomb theory seems extremely weak.

The Hallucination Theory

Some critics contend that the resurrection of Christ occurred solely in the minds of the disciples. Dr. William McNeil articulates this position in his book, *A World History:*

> The Roman authorities in Jerusalem arrested and crucified Jesus. . . . But soon afterwards the dispirited Apostles gathered in an upstairs room and *suddenly felt* again the heartwarming presence of their master. This seemed absolutely convincing evidence that Jesus' death on the cross had not been the end but the beginning. . . . The Apostles bubbled over with excitement and tried to explain to all who would listen all that had happened.[3] (italics added)

This position, that Jesus' appearance was a feeling rather than an actuality, is untenable for several reasons. For hallucinations of this type to occur, psychiatrists agree, several conditions must exist. First, the people to whom hallucinations occur are generally of an imaginative or nervous disposition. Although the eleven remaining disciples had been experiencing anxiety and grief before the Resurrection, they were not what one would consider imaginative or highly strung individuals. Rather, they were, practical and pragmatic working men who were concerned with the cares of every day existence. Consider, too, their lack of imagination and vision during the time of Jesus' ministry. For the most part, they didn't grasp who Jesus was or what His work entailed.

Second, it is highly unlikely that the same hallucination would occur in the way described in Scripture. Jesus appeared a number of times, in a variety of locations, and to different people.

Third, because hallucinations are subjective to each individual, it is unlikely that in a group hallucination experience each person would have the exact same hallucinatory vision. Paul mentions an instance when more than five hundred people saw the exact same thing at the same time—the resurrected Christ. Paul added, incidentally, that some of the eyewitnesses were still alive and could verify what he said (1 Cor. 15:5–7).

Finally, hallucinations of this nature generally occur to those who intensely *want* to believe. But one of the disciples, Thomas, was skeptical of the news of the Resurrection and wanted more proof. Jesus gave it to him (John 20:24–29). Perhaps some of the other disciples had their doubts as well. Thomas's experience was not a hallucination, and its inclusion in the account by John doesn't help the hallucination theory.

Proponents of the hallucination theory must still account for the empty tomb. If the apostles hallucinated the Resurrection that they were preaching, the authorities needed only to produce the body, and that would have ended the apostles' claims.

The Swoon Theory

A third theory argues that Jesus didn't actually die on the cross; He merely passed out from His pain and injuries and was mistakenly assumed to be dead. In reality, goes the argument, He revived after three days, exited the tomb, and appeared to His disciples, who believed that He had risen from the dead. This theory was developed in the early nineteenth century but today has been completely discounted for several reasons.

First, it is a physical impossibility that Jesus could have survived the tortures of the crucifixion. Second, the soldiers who crucified Jesus were experts in carrying out this type of execution, and they took precautions to ensure that He actually was dead. When they thrust a spear into His side, blood and water, as the written account states, came out separately, an indication that blood cells had already begun to separate from the plasma, which occurs only when blood stops circulating. Furthermore, Roman executioners routinely broke the legs of crucified criminals to speed the process of dying. This act was not performed upon Jesus. The soldiers saw no need to do so after they had examined His body carefully and concluded that He was already dead.

After being taken down from the cross, Jesus was prepared for burial, which involved wrapping the corpse in linen cloth layered with many pounds of spices. To believe that after three days with no food or water Jesus would revive is unreasonable. Even harder to believe is that Jesus could roll a two-ton stone up an incline, overpower the guards, and then walk several miles to Emmaus. Even if Jesus had done all of this—appeared to the disciples, half-dead and desperately in need of medical attention—His doing so would not have prompted their worship of Him as God.

In the nineteenth century, David F. Strauss, an opponent of Christianity, fatally discredited the swoon theory:

> It is impossible that a being who had stolen half-dead out of the sepulchre, who crept about weak and ill, wanting medical treatment, who required bandaging, strengthening, and indulgence, and who still at last yielded to his sufferings, could have given the disciples the impression that he was a Conqueror over death and the grave, the Prince of life, an impression that would lay at the bottom of their future ministry.[4]

Although Strauss did not believe in the Resurrection, he nonetheless considered the swoon theory to be outlandish.

The Stolen-Body Theory

This fourth argument holds that either the disciples or the Jewish (or Roman) authorities stole or moved the body for safekeeping. Consider the first possibility—that the disciples stole the body. Unless the Roman guards were asleep (see the section titled "Soldiers-Fell-Asleep Theory"), the disciples would have had to first overpower the guards, an unlikely scenario in light of the fact that the disciples had fled in terror two days before and had been in fear for their lives ever since.

But if the disciples had stolen the body, why would

they deceive their own people into believing in a false Messiah? The disciples knew that being a follower of Christ would mean death for hundreds of their believing friends. Why, then, would the disciples proclaim a false message throughout the Roman world and give their lives in martyrdom for this lie? On the other hand, if the Jews or the Romans had the body, why did they accuse the disciples of stealing it (Matt. 28:11–15)? In Acts 4, the Jewish authorities were angered and did everything they could to prevent the spread of Christianity. If the Jews or the Romans knew where the body was, they would have produced it as soon as the apostles began to preach their new message in Jerusalem, ending the matter that had caused them so much trouble and embarrassment. But no historical evidence indicates that the authorities refuted the Resurrection by producing the body. This stolen-body theory is self-contradictory and has little merit.

The Soldiers-Fell-Asleep Theory

The fifth theory has existed since the very day of Christ's resurrection and is still believed now by many opponents of Christianity. Matthew 28:12–13 articulates this position as follows:

> When the chief priests had met with the elders and devised a plan, they gave the soldiers a large sum of money, telling them, "You are to say, 'His disciples came during the night and stole him away *while we were asleep.*'" (NIV, italics added)

Many people have wondered why Matthew records this conspiracy and then does not refute it. Perhaps it was because the very idea is so preposterous that he saw no need for a defense. This theory remains an impossibility for several reasons. First, if the soldiers were sleeping, how did they know it was the disciples who stole the body? Second, it would seem physically impossible for the disciples to sneak past the soldiers and then move a two-ton stone up an incline in absolute silence. Surely the guards would have heard something.

Third, the tomb was secured with a Roman seal (Matt. 27:66). Anyone who moved the stone would break the seal, an offense punishable by death. The depression and cowardice of the disciples make it difficult to believe that they would suddenly become so brave as to face a detachment of Roman soldiers, steal the body, and then lie about the Resurrection, fully knowing that they would ultimately face a life of suffering and the threat of death as a result of their contrived message.

Fourth, Roman guards were not likely to fall asleep with such an important duty. Severe penalties were prescribed for those soldiers who did so.

Finally, the gospel of John says that the grave clothes were found "lying there, as well as the burial cloth that had been around Jesus' head. The cloth was folded up by itself separate from the linen" (20:6–7 NIV). Imagine a group of men, untrained in combat skills, sneaking past sleeping armed guards, who *were* trained in combat skills. First, the disciples would have had to roll away the stone, fearful with every moment of awakening the guards. Then we are to believe that they took the time to unwrap the body and fold the headpiece neatly next to the linen. The disciples would far more likely have flung down the garments in disorder—or taken the body, wrappings and all—and fled for fear of detection.

Monumental Implications

These five theories inadequately account for the empty tomb, the transformation of the apostles, and the birth of Christianity in the city of the Crucifixion. One must seriously consider, then, that Jesus rose from the grave. The implications of this conclusion are monumental.

First, if Jesus rose from the dead, then what He said about Himself is true: "I am the resurrection and the life; he who believes in Me shall live even if he dies" (John 11:25), and "I am the way, and the truth, and the life; no man comes to the Father, but through Me" (John 14:6). If the Resurrection is true, if Jesus is God, then eternal life is found through Jesus Christ alone. Any religious belief that contradicts this claim must be false. All religious leaders have been buried in some grave, but the grave of Jesus is empty because He is not there; He has risen!

The second implication is expressed by Paul in 1 Corinthians 15:54: "Death has been swallowed up in victory" (NIV). Physical death is not the end; eternal life with our Lord awaits all who trust in Him because Jesus has conquered death.

Additional Reading:

Craig, William Lane. *Apologetics: An Introduction.* Chicago: Moody, 1984.

Geisler, Norman L., and Ronald M. Brooks. *When Skeptics Ask: A Handbook on Christian Evidences.* Wheaton, Ill.: Victor Books, 1990.

Greenleaf, Simon. *The Testimony of the Evangelists: The Gospels Examined by the Rules of Evidence.* Grand Rapids: Kregel, 1995.

Little, Paul. *Know Why You Believe.* Downers Grove, Ill.: InterVarsity, 1968.

McDowell, Josh. *Evidence that Demands a Verdict.* San Bernardino, Calif.: Here's Life Publishers, 1979.

————. *The Resurrection Factor.* San Bernardino, Calif.: Here's Life Publishers, 1981.

McNeil, William. *A World History.* 3d ed. New York: Oxford University Press, 1979.

Montgomery, John W. *Evidence for Faith.* Dallas: Probe Books, 1991.

Morison, Frank. *Who Moved the Stone?* Grand Rapids: Zondervan, 1958.

Strauss, David. *The Life of Jesus for the People.* Vol. 1. 2d ed. London: Williams and Norgate, 1879.

15

A Moral Life Won't Get Us to Heaven

Jimmy Williams

This final chapter concerns the question, "Won't a good, moral life get me to heaven?" We will consider several crucial issues related to this question.

Man: The Only Animal Who Worships

The first issue concerns the very nature of human beings. One of the most remarkable things about humans is that from the dawn of our history, in all places on this planet, we have participated in worshiping. Humans are, in fact, the only animals in the world who worship, and we seem to be incurably religious. Why do we worship, and how do those reasons bear on the question of having good morals and getting to heaven?

Some foundational elements seem to be universals when it comes to human religious behavior. The first universal, as was stated earlier, is that humans do, indeed, worship—a phenomenon that implies a second universal: We assume the existence of a being who is worthy of that worship. Ethnic groups of all kinds and in all places, whether remote or in close proximity to other peoples, have their own history, folklore, deities, rituals, particular moral systems, and life-customs, all of which are intended to enable people to cope with the passages of life—from childhood to maturity to old age and to the ultimate arrival at that dark gate, *death.* Christians directly relate this human inclination to worship to *Imago Dei*—that is, human beings are created in God's divine image.

The second universal is how and what humans worship. The most prominent feature of human worship from its earliest beginnings has been a sacrifice—whether the sheep, goats, or bulls of the early Mediterranean world; the human beings that the Polynesians hurled into the mouths of volcanoes; the child sacrifices of the Canaanites; or the ritual slaughter practiced by the Aztecs, the Incas, and virtually all of the other New World Indians. In all cases, apparently, some kind of blood must flow. We can add to this fact the prominence (in many cultures) of self-sacrifice through flagellation, severe asceticism, or other acts of personal penance.

The centrality of sacrifice in all religious thinking points to a third universal: Humans sense that one being exists to whom they are accountable for their behavior. We also sense a fourth universal—guilt, the sense that we have fallen short of what that higher being (or beings) requires of us, that *God is not pleased with me.* People worship because they feel guilty. They feel this guilt because they perceive that they have fallen short of the standard that God, others, and they themselves require.

Humans, then, have a sense that we are accountable to some higher authority for our conduct. Therefore, we offer sacrifice to gain divine favor and to avoid personal guilt and punishment. We continually worship to resolve our inner conflict of feeling estranged from God because of our sin. These universal human religious behaviors provide the bases for considering the original question: Is a good, moral life sufficient to assure someone a place in heaven?

The Great Global Heresy: Religion

"Good children go to heaven, and bad children go to hell!"

Many of us at one time or another have experienced a parent or a teacher who pointed a finger at us and warned of the ultimate outcome of our behavior. This "Santa Claus" mentality suggests that God is "making a list and checking it twice, gonna find out who's naughty or nice."

This kind of religion is, in fact, the most popular approach to God on the planet. And we are familiar with jokes about the person who dies and stands face to face with Saint Peter at the golden gates of heaven. Peter stands ready to evaluate and pass judgment on whether we've been good enough to be admitted. Saint Peter expects each of us to give a moral account of ourselves before we are allowed inside. The general, world-wide assumption is that our good deeds and our bad deeds are to be placed on the divine scales and weighed at the time of physical death to determine if we go "up" or "down." In Christianity's viewpoint, however, this perception represents a great, global heresy.

The "divine scales" perception is "religion," but it is definitely not Christianity. Christianity is, in fact, radically opposed to such an idea, insisting that not what we *do* but rather what has already been *done* on our behalf gets us to heaven. The global heresy, which many people call religion, actually has its origin in Hinduism. God resides at the top of a great mountain, so goes the idea, and it makes little difference which path a seeker chooses in his or her ascent; all paths lead to the God at the top. And "religion" says that it is up to *you* to climb if you want to reach the summit . . . and God.

At the western end of the Forum in ancient Rome, stood the *Millenarium Aureum,* the Golden Milestone. Augustus Caesar erected this gilded bronze column to mark the junction and the origin of the major Roman roads, which spread out like the spokes of a great wheel in every direction to distant destinations throughout the Roman Empire. On this column were inscribed the major towns and their distances from Rome, giving rise to the popular saying, "All roads lead to Rome." Religious pluralists could be said to have adopted a similar saying in regard to God: "It doesn't matter what you believe. It's important only that you sincerely try to do your best. We're all trying to get to the same place, and we all worship the same God . . . and all religions lead to the same God."

But the Genesis account of Adam and Eve depicts a far different approach to God. In fact, only one approach is judged to be acceptable. After Adam and Eve disobeyed God, they hid in the bushes and fashioned fig leaves to cover their nakedness. God looked at the fig leaves, and He was not pleased. He scolded their disobedience and their efforts to cover themselves. Adam and Eve had not only to admit their guilt and disobedience but also to acknowledge their inability to make things right through their own efforts. They could neither cover over nor atone for what they had done. The account says that God took the initiative. He killed some animals, which were in essence sacrificed for their skins to cover Adam and Eve.

All philosophies, religions, asceticism, ethics, philanthropic activities, and any other system that seeks the approval of God through human self-effort are versions of the "fig-leaf" approach. They represent the core of what we call religion, the best effort of human beings to find God. But every worshiper encounters a problem. Consider the mountain-climbing metaphor that was introduced earlier. When one is climbing that mountain to approach God, he or she encounters an impenetrable barrier that denies further advance—the barrier of God's holiness and perfection. Each individual's personal sin and imperfection prevents him or her from approaching God.

The Problem of Sin

What constitutes the sin problem, and what are the eternal consequences of sin for each individual? When the word *sin* comes up in a conversation, most people cringe or avert their eyes. We *do* a lot of it; we just don't like to *talk* about it! And many people cannot even define *sin* or *sinner*. Sin is a violation of God's Law, the standard that God requires of every human. A sinner, therefore, is someone who has broken or fallen short of that standard.

Don't misunderstand me. I'm not saying that there's no good at all in people. There's a great deal of good in people. Most people are not as bad as they *could* be. The point is, if being good gets us to heaven, how much good is good enough? Many people say that they try to live by the Ten Commandments or by some other rule of life, such as the Golden Rule. And yet, if we are honest, we must admit that we've violated our own standards at some point. Such was Paul's meaning when he said, "All have sinned and fall short of the glory of God" (Rom. 3:23). The Scriptures are clear—God does not demand goodness. Adam and Eve's best efforts to cover themselves were not good enough. The good that is in humans, all of our moral achievement, is not acceptable to God because God does not demand goodness; He demands perfection!

To demonstrate how far from perfection are human beings, consider that the Grand Canyon is six miles across at its narrowest. The longest distance a human being has been able to jump is 29 feet, 4 1/2 inches, a world record set by Mike Powell at the 1991 world track-and-field championships in Tokyo. Yet, a person is more likely to jump across the Grand Canyon than to establish fellowship with God through his or her own efforts. To establish such fellowship, the standard we humans must meet is God's perfection. Who can do that? It's a goal so distant that no one could reach it.

The goal becomes even more distant when we understand that, as James tells us, "whoever keeps the whole law and yet stumbles in one point, he has become guilty of all" (James 2:10). Therefore, someone who breaks just one of the commandments is as guilty as if he or she had broken all ten!

But God did not give the Ten Commandments because He knew that human beings would keep them perfectly. Rather, the Bible tells us that He gave us the Ten Commandments to reveal something. Consider an X-ray machine. The machine reveals the condition of a broken arm, but it will not set and knit the bones, nor will it put the arm in a cast. By the same token, the Ten Commandments reveal to us the condition of our lives, but they cannot heal us, change us, or cover our sin.

The Pharisees looked at the Law and then at their own lives and said, "I'm pretty good, *really* good." Jesus had wanted them to come to the opposite conclusion. He even called them hypocrites, saying that they were wrong to claim that they were righteous and that all was well between them and their Maker. "It is not those who are healthy who need a physician," Jesus said, "but those who are sick" (Matt. 9:12). When you think that you are well, you don't seek a doctor. Only when you realize that you are sick do you consult a physician. Jesus was urging the Pharisees to be honest about themselves: "I did not come to call the righteous, but sinners" (v. 13).

When my wife, Carol, and I travel, and I discover that I'm lost, I resist her suggestion, "Why don't you ask for directions?" In my case, my resistance stems from male pride. With the Pharisees, their resistance to Jesus' message was based on religious pride, as is the case for all who would seek heaven on the basis of their own merits. A wise old Baptist preacher once said, "It isn't difficult to get people saved; it is difficult to get them *lost!*" This is the dilemma of all humanity: Like the Pharisees, people cling to the old fig leaves of self-effort instead of submitting to the covering that God Himself has provided for all (Christ's sacrificial death on the cross). Each of us must choose one or the other (John 3:18, 36).

The Problem of Righteousness

When we feel the sting of guilt for our own sin, we, like Adam and Eve, try to do something about it. Although morality and human goodness are to be commended, God makes clear that no one, through his or her own efforts, can make himself or herself presentable before God. Charles Haddon Spurgeon once suggested that people are basically like silkworms, busily spinning to clothe themselves but actually spinning a shroud wrapping for themselves.

Our problem is not only that we fall short of God's standard by sinning (Rom. 3:23) but also we lack something. We need not only the removal of personal sin through blood sacrifice to satisfy divine justice but also something further to make us fit for heaven. Isaiah spoke of this unfitness: "For all of us have become like one who is unclean, and all our righteous deeds are like a filthy garment" (Isa. 64:6). Not only our sins but also even our good deeds are unacceptable. We need not only atonement for our sins but also righteousness to enter heaven. But it has to be a certain kind of righteousness.

The Pharisees were considered to be the most righteous people of Jesus' day. They knew the Old Testament by heart. They went to the synagogue three times a day and prayed seven times a day. They were respected in the community. But Jesus looked through their religious veneer and, in their presence, admonished the crowds that "unless your righteousness surpasses that of the scribes and Pharisees, you shall not enter the kingdom of heaven" (Matt. 5:20).

When the crowds heard this, they stared at each other in bewilderment. "You mean the Pharisees aren't righteous enough to go to heaven? If *they* can't make it, who will?"

We first observe the conflict between these two kinds of righteousness in the Garden of Eden: (1) human righteousness, which is symbolized by the fig leaves that Adam and Eve used to cover themselves and be presentable before God, and (2) divine righteousness, which is symbolized by the adequate covering of the slain animal skins provided by God Himself. We find these two kinds of righteousness clashing all the way through both Old and New Testaments, and they remain with us today. Paul was fully aware of both when he spoke of his Jewish brethren: "I bear them witness that they have a zeal for God, but not in accordance with knowledge. For not knowing about God's righteousness, and seeking to establish their own [righteousness], they did not subject themselves to the righteousness of God" (Rom. 10:2–3).

Think of these two kinds of righteousness mathematically. Call God's righteousness $+R$ and human righteousness $-R$. The first righteousness is absolute whereas the second righteousness is relative. Over a lifetime, a human being can accumulate a huge pile of $-R$, but added up, it still totals $-R$.

In the former Soviet Union, rubles are printed and circulated. With those rubles, you can buy your dinner, pay your hotel bill, and purchase goods in the shops. But if you tried to use rubles in America, they would not be honored. It would be futile to try to pay with rubles in America.

To do business with God in heaven, we must deal with Him in the only currency that He honors and accepts, and that is $+R$. To try to negotiate with God on the basis of relative human goodness is futile. We need $+R$.

Where do we get such currency? It is given to us as a gift if we will accept it—the perfect righteousness of Jesus Christ. The yardstick by which God measures everyone is His Son. This $+R$ righteousness is ours only in Christ: "He saved us, not on the basis of deeds which we have done in righteousness, but according to His mercy, by the washing of regeneration and renewing by the Holy Spirit" (Titus 3:5). This gracious provision is a radical departure from all other religious ideas that humans have ever conceived. It is so radical, in fact, that human beings would never have thought of it.

The Uniqueness of Christian Grace

This chapter has sought a biblical answer to the question, "Will a good, moral life get me to heaven?" We have examined the bankruptcy of every attempt by people to reach that goal through self-effort. We have discovered that the salvation offered by Christianity is uniquely opposed to all human efforts to secure redemption by working one's way into God's good graces. If, in fact, God expected us to attain our salvation through good deeds, then He made a terrible mistake. He allowed His only-begotten Son to come to earth—robed in human flesh—and die a horrible death on a cross. If good works constitute the path to God, then God allowed His Son to die for nothing. But Jesus died for our personal, eternal benefit. Seeking any other way to heaven is to disavow totally the significance of Christ's death, making it meaningless and unnecessary.

What God offers us is free. It is a gift, which none of us deserves, nor could we ever repay what the gift is worth. God has dealt with humankind in grace and love. The only thing that God has asked of us is that we humbly admit that we have broken His laws, acknowledge that He has indeed made things right through His Son's sacrificial death on the cross, and accept His forgiveness by faith. We are invited to lay aside our own fig leaves and submit freely to the covering that God has provided for us through His crucified Son, the very righteousness of Christ.

This message is what Jesus sought to communicate in Matthew 22:1–14, the parable about the wedding feast that a king was preparing to give his son:

> And those slaves went out into the streets, and gathered together all they found, both evil and good; and the wedding hall was filled with dinner guests. But when the king came in to look over the dinner

guests, he saw there a man not dressed in wedding clothes, and he said to him, "Friend, how did you come in here without wedding clothes?" And he was speechless. Then the king said to the servants, "Bind him hand and foot, and cast him into the outer darkness; in that place there shall be weeping and gnashing of teeth." (vv. 10–13)

The text doesn't tell us whether this person was one of the "good" ones or one of the "evil" ones; that detail is irrelevant to what Jesus wants us to understand. The importance lies in the proper attire for the occasion. God is telling us that the only acceptable attire for heaven is the righteousness of Christ. As a gracious host, He stands holding out to humanity the most costly garment in the universe, and He eagerly desires to wrap us in it—safe and warm and happy and secure: "I will rejoice greatly in the LORD, my soul will exult in my God; for He has clothed me with garments of salvation, He has wrapped me with a robe of righteousness, as a bridegroom decks himself with a garland, and as a bride adorns herself with her jewels" (Isa. 61:10).

A Prayer Away

Everything that needed to be done for your salvation and mine was accomplished the moment Christ died on the cross. The penalty for sin has been paid, and God's righteous demands for holiness have been satisfied. God is now free to extend His love and eternal life as a free gift. He declares, "The wages of sin is death, but the free gift of God is eternal life in Christ Jesus our Lord" (Rom. 6:23).

Gifts, of course, must be received. For that reason, Jesus said, "He who believes has eternal life" (John 6:47). *Believe* means "to trust or depend upon." God is asking each person to come as a sinner to Him. He asks us to recognize that His Son died on the cross for us, and to trust His Son *alone* as our only hope of heaven.

This was the message, the Good News that the first Christians took to the world: "And there is salvation in no one else; for there is no other name under heaven that has been given among men, by which we must be saved" (Acts 4:12).

Every human being is just a prayer away from receiving the grace and forgiveness of God and the promise of heaven. But that prayer must be the right prayer and be based on the right facts, that Jesus Christ came into this world to save sinners, not "do-gooders": "I did not come to call the righteous, but sinners" (Matt. 9:13).

You can begin today to trust Christ for your salvation, instead of your own futile efforts at trying to be a fairly nice person all of your life. Obviously, your heart attitude and your sincerity count. God knows your heart. If the following suggested prayer will help to bring a sense of closure and certainty to your decision to believe in and to trust Christ, then please feel free to use it as a guide:

> Dear God, I admit that I am a sinner, and nothing I can do will ever get me to heaven. But I believe that Jesus Christ died for me and rose from the grave to prove the validity of His claim to be my Savior. He took my place and my punishment. So, right now, I place my trust in Christ alone to make me presentable and acceptable to You. Come into my life. I accept the gift of Your Son. Thank You that You are now within me. I know that this fact is not based upon my feelings but upon Your prom-

ise. If I open the door of my life and invite You to come live within me and be my Savior (Rev. 3:20; John 1:12) you will make me the kind of person You want me to be. Begin to show me that You really have entered my life and heart, and now give me the guidance that I need to live a new life in fellowship with You. Amen.

Endnotes

Chapter 2: Does God Exist?

1. *Webster's New Collegiate Dictionary* (Springfield, Mass.: G. & C. Merriam, 1953), s.v. "metaphysics."
2. Anthony Kenny, *Five Ways* (London: Routledge Kegan Paul, 1969), 66.
3. Carl Sagan, *Cosmos* (New York: Random House, 1980), 4.
4. David Hume, *An Enquiry: Concerning Human Understanding,* Great Books of the Western World, vol. 35 (Chicago: William Benton, 1952), 506.
5. Robert Jastrow, *God and the Astronomers* (New York: W. W. Norton, 1978), 94–95.
6. Ibid., 15.
7. Ibid., 109.
8. Robert Jastrow, "A Scientist Caught Between Two Faiths," interview by Bill Durbin, *Christianity Today,* 26 (6 August 1982): 14–18.
9. Walter L. Bradley, "Is There Scientific Evidence for an Intelligent Creator of the Universe?" (lecture given at High Ground Men's Conference, Beaver Creek, Colo., 2 March 2001), 1.
10. C. S. Lewis, *Mere Christianity* (New York: MacMillan, 1943), 18.
11. Ibid., 45.
12. Ibid., 70–71.
13. *Webster's New Collegiate Dictionary,* s.v. "agnosticism."
14. Leith Samuel, *Impossibility of Agnosticism* (Downers Grove, Ill: InterVarsity, n.d.).

Chapter 3: The Problem of Evil

1. John R. W. Stott, *The Cross of Christ* (Downers Grove, Ill.: InterVarsity, 1986), 311.

2. The pantheistic perspective on evil is discussed fully by David K. Clark and Norman L. Geisler, *Apologetics in the New Age: A Christian Critique of Pantheism* (Grand Rapids: Baker, 1990), chap. 10.

3. For an explanation of this fact, see Peter Kreeft, *Making Sense Out of Suffering* (Ann Arbor, Mich.: Servant Books, 1986). He says on page 31, "[I]f there is no God, no infinite goodness, where did we get the idea of evil? Where did we get the standard of goodness by which we judge evil as evil?"

4. This view is set forth in the popular book by Rabbi Harold Kushner, *When Bad Things Happen to Good People* (New York: Avon, 1983).

5. The writer of this chapter acknowledges his debt to many other authors who have analyzed the problem of evil in much greater depth, and who have described the commonly used categories and approaches referred to in both the preceding and the following contexts. The ideas expressed in the following sections reflect largely the writings of the following authors: William Lane Craig, *No Easy Answers: Finding Hope in Doubt, Failure, and Unanswered Prayer* (Chicago: Moody, 1990), chaps. 4 and 5; Norman L. Geisler, *Philosophy of Religion* (Grand Rapids: Zondervan, 1974), chaps. 14–17; Michael Peterson, William Hasker, Bruce Reichenbach, and David Basinger, *Reason and Religious Belief: An Introduction to the Philosophy of Religion* (New York and Oxford: Oxford University Press, 1991); and Alvin C. Plantinga, *God, Freedom, and Evil* (Grand Rapids: Eerdmans, 1974).

6. For a fuller explanation, see Plantinga, *God, Freedom, and Evil,* 29–53.

7. This argument, known as the "Free Will Defense," has been most thoroughly set forth in Plantinga's book, *God, Freedom, and Evil.*

8. Geisler writes, "[A] world with the greater number of moral virtues is morally better than one with a lesser number of them. And certain virtues like courage, fortitude, mercy, and forgiveness are attainable only in a world where sin occurs" (*Philosophy of Religion,* 361).

9. See Plantinga, *God, Freedom, and Evil,* 58.

10. Sheldon Vanauken, foreword to *Making Sense Out of Suffering,* by Peter Kreeft (Ann Arbor, Mich.: Servant, 1986), viii.

11. For a more complete discussion of the evidential problem of evil, see Craig, *No Easy Answers,* chapter 5. Some of the following discussion reflects his thought in this chapter.

12. "There is a difference between our knowing the purpose for evil and God having a purpose for it." Norman L. Geisler and Ronald M. Brooks, *When Skeptics Ask: A Handbook on Christian Evidences* (Wheaton, Ill.: Victor, 1990), 65.

13. For a balanced discussion of the role of grief in the Christian's life, see J. A. Motyer, *The Message of Philippians* (Downers Grove, Ill.: InterVarsity, 1984), 88–90. "Tears are proper for believers—indeed they should be all the more copious, for Christians are more sensitively aware of every emotion, whether of joy or sorrow, than those who have known nothing of the softening and enlivening grace of God. . . . These two 'poles' of confidence and tears should mark our attitude to death. . . . We face our own death with triumphant assurance, but surely not without a pang for all we enjoy in this life and which will then be past for ever. We face the death of our loved ones with triumph, but surely not without a tear because they are gone." The aim of the Holy Spirit is to *sanctify* human emotion, rather than to eliminate it.

14. Stott says, "There is good biblical evidence that God not only suffered in Christ, but that God in Christ suffers with his people still" (*The Cross of Christ*, 335). See also the comments by Joni Eareckson Tada and Steven Estes in *When God Weeps: Why Our Sufferings Matter to the Almighty* (Grand Rapids: Zondervan, 1997): "As with human sin, so with human sorrow—*many* passages elaborate on how it touches God's heart" (244). "God does look down on his world and weep. But its twistedness did not catch him by surprise. He knew that humans would fall into sin. He knew the immeasurable sorrow this would let loose. He knew the suffering it would cost his own Son. But he decreed to permit this fall because he knew how he would resolve it: that Jesus would die, that his church would eventually triumph through innumerable trials. . . . *God sees this glorious end as clearly as if it were today.* . . . This, in our opinion, is how he can be truly 'blessed,' and truly weep" (248).

15. Henri Blocher, *Evil and the Cross* (Downers Grove, Ill.: InterVarsity, 1994), 132.

16. The idea that this life is "the best possible *way to* the best possible world" is fully discussed in Geisler, *Philosophy of Religion,* chaps. 14–17. Concerning the permanence of the good use of free choice in heaven by the saints, Geisler has this to say: "All the lessons of why freedom without evil is better than freedom with evil are being preserved by God and will ultimately be applied by Him to the whole race in order to convince them of the wrongness of evil. Then, when the infinitely persuasive good of God's nature is revealed, it will not violate but perfect the freedom to do good which free choice to do evil has shown is the only proper good for free creatures" (369).

17. Havergal's poem is cited without reference in Gary Crandall's book,

Gold Under Fire: The Christian and Adversity (Winona Lake, Ind.: BMH, 1992), 185–86.

Chapter 4: Is Jesus the Only Savior?

1. Erwin Lutzer draws an important distinction among three kinds of "tolerance" in his book *Christ Among Other Gods* (Chicago: Moody, 1994), 29. *Legal tolerance* is recognition that each person has the right to believe whatever he or she determines is true or best. *Social tolerance* is recognition that people should be treated with dignity and respect, regardless of their religious beliefs. *Uncritical tolerance* is the idea that no religious belief should be evaluated as false or inferior to any other religious beliefs. Although legal and social tolerance should be granted to everyone, uncritical tolerance demands a price that is too great to pay—the sacrifice of the concept of truth itself.

2. Although religious pluralism has had advocates since even ancient times, its foremost proponent in our generation has been John Hick. His ideas are most completely set forth in his books *An Interpretation of Religion* (New Haven, Conn.: Yale University Press, 1989); and *A Christian Theology of Religions* (Louisville: Westminster John Knox, 1995).

3. An example of this kind of thinking can be found in Frithjof Schuon, *The Transcendent Unity of Religions* (New York: Harper and Row, 1975).

4. This is the position of Hick, *An Interpretation of Religion,* chapters 17–18.

5. John Hick, *God Has Many Names* (Philadelphia: Westminster, 1982), 19.

6. This view has had many advocates through the centuries and continues to find support. Among evangelicals, the most outspoken recent proponent has been Clark Pinnock. See his *A Wideness in God's Mercy: The Finality of Jesus Christ in a World of Religions* (Grand Rapids: Zondervan, 1992).

7. This was the view set forth, for example, in James Denney, *Studies in Theology,* 3d ed. (London: Hodder and Stoughton, 1895), 243.

8. For a discussion of these contrasts, see Norman Anderson, *Christianity and World Religions: The Challenge of Pluralism* (Downers Grove, Ill.: InterVarsity, 1984), 58f., 107, 111.

9. For an excellent exposition of passages in 1 Peter, see Edmund Clowney, *The Message of 1 Peter* (Downers Grove, Ill.: InterVarsity, 1988), 161–64, 175–76.

Chapter 5: Apologetics and Evangelism

1. W. E. Vine, *An Expository Dictionary of New Testament Words* (Old Tappan, N.J.: Revell, 1959), 179.

2. J. Gresham Machen, *Christianity and Culture* (Princeton, N.J.: Princeton Theological Review 11, 1913), 7.

Chapter 6: Are the Biblical Documents Reliable?

1. C. Sanders, *An Introduction to Research in English Literary History* (New York: Macmillan, 1952), 143.
2. Geza Vermes, *The Completed Dead Sea Scrolls in English* (New York: Penguin Press, 1997), 321.
3. Merrill F. Unger, *Famous Archaeological Discoveries* (Grand Rapids: Zondervan, 1957), 72.
4. Paul Little, *Know Why You Believe* (Downer's Grove, Ill.: InterVarsity, 1968), 41.
5. R. Laird Harris, *Can I Trust My Bible?* (Chicago: Moody, 1963), 124.
6. Ibid., 129–30.
7. Merrill F. Unger, *Unger's Bible Handbook* (Chicago, Moody, 1967), 892.
8. Ibid.
9. Ibid.
10. Sir Fredric Kenyon, *The Bible and Archaeology* (New York: Harper & Brothers, 1940), 288ff.
11. B. F. Wescott and F. J. A. Hort, eds., *New Testament in Original Greek,* vol. 2 (London: R. F. Weymouth, 1886), 2.

Chapter 7: Is the Bible Inspired?

1. Carl F. H. Henry, *God Who Speaks and Shows,* vol. 4 of *God, Revelation and Authority* (Waco, Tex.: Word, 1979), 129.
2. Carl F. H. Henry, "Introduction to Theology," class notes, Trinity Evangelical Divinity School, 4 May 1987. See also Benjamin Breckinridge Warfield, cited in Henry, *God Who Speaks and Shows,* 4:141.
3. L. Gaussen, *The Inspiration of the Holy Scriptures* (Chicago: Moody, 1949), 145. See the entire section, pp. 145–52.
4. Benjamin Breckinridge Warfield, *The Inspiration and Authority of the Bible* (Phillipsburg, N.J.: Presbyterian and Reformed Publishing, 1948), 107.
5. Ibid., 108–9.
6. Ibid., 110–11.
7. Rene Paché, *The Inspiration and Authority of Scripture* (Chicago: Moody, 1969), 81.
8. John W. Wenham, *Christ and the Bible* (Downers Grove, Ill.: InterVarsity, 1972), 24.

9. Robert P. Lightner, *The Savior and the Scriptures* (Nutley, N.J.: Presbyterian and Reformed Publishing, 1970), 28–29. See also Paché, *The Inspiration and Authority of Scripture,* 217–21.

10. Wenham, *Christ and the Bible,* 113.

11. Herman Ridderbos, "The Canon of the New Testament," in *Revelation and the Bible,* ed. Carl F. H. Henry (Grand Rapids: Baker, 1958), 192–93.

12. Ibid., 193.

13. Edward J. Young, *Thy Word Is Truth* (Grand Rapids: Eerdmans, 1957), 21.

14. For help in dealing with relativism and religious pluralism, see the Probe Web site (www.probe.com): "How Do You Spell Truth?" by Don Closson, and chapter 4 in this book, "Is Jesus the Only Savior?" by Rick Rood.

15. Josh McDowell, *Evidence that Demands a Verdict* (San Bernardino, Calif.: Here's Life Publishers, 1979), 144.

16. See Bernard Ramm, *Protestant Christian Evidences* (Chicago: Moody, 1953), esp. chaps. 8 and 9.

Chapter 8: The Christian Canon

1. Louis Berkhof, *The History of Christian Doctrines* (Carlisle, Pa.: Banner of Truth, 1937), 37.

2. John D. Hannah, lecture notes from History of Doctrine class, Dallas Theological Seminary, Dallas, Tex., lesson 2, page 2.

3. Berkhof, *The History of Christian Doctrines,* 39.

4. Norman L. Geisler, *Decide for Yourself: How History Views the Bible* (Grand Rapids: Zondervan, 1982), 11.

5. Berkhof, *The History of Christian Doctrines,* 54.

6. Hannah, lecture notes from History of Doctrine class, lesson 2, page 5.

7. Geisler, *Decide for Yourself,* 12.

8. Hannah, lecture notes from History of Doctrine class, lesson 2, page 6.

9. Ibid., lesson 3, page 3.

10. Ibid., lesson 3, page 7.

11. John Calvin, *Institutes of the Christian Religion* (Philadelphia: Westminster, 1977), 80.

12. Ibid.

13. Hannah, lecture notes from History of Doctrine class, lesson 4, page 2.

14. Ibid., lesson 4, page 5.

15. Peter C. Hodgson and Robert H. King, eds., *Christian Theology: An Introduction to Its Traditions and Tasks* (Philadelphia: Fortress, 1985), 1–2.

16. Ibid., 27.

17. William Lane Craig, *Reasonable Faith: Christian Truth and Apologetics* (Wheaton, Ill.: Crossway Books, 1994). See Craig's discussion of faith and reason in chapter 1.

Chapter 9: The Old Testament and the Apocrypha

1. F. F. Bruce, *The Canon of Scripture* (Downers Grove, Ill.: InterVarsity, 1988), 43.
2. Ibid., 45.
3. Gleason L. Archer, *A Survey of Old Testament Introduction* (Chicago: Moody, 1974), 73.
4. Merrill F. Unger, *Introductory Guide to the Old Testament* (Grand Rapids: Zondervan, 1970), 99.
5. Archer, *A Survey of Old Testament Introduction,* 73.
6. Bruce, *The Canon of Scripture,* 49.
7. Ibid., 72. (Ezra and Nehemiah were often combined into one book, as were Lamentations and Jeremiah and the twelve Minor Prophets).
8. Ibid., 87.
9. Ibid., 90.
10. Christopher A. Hall, *Reading Scripture with the Church Fathers* (Downers Grove, Ill.: InterVarsity, 1998), 187.
11. Ibid.
12. Ibid.
13. Norman L. Geisler, *Baker Encyclopedia of Christian Apologetics* (Grand Rapids: Baker, 1999), 85.
14. Ibid., 32.
15. Unger, *Introductory Guide to the Old Testament,* 109–11.
16. Geisler, *Baker Encyclopedia of Christian Apologetics,* 31.

Chapter 10: The Debate over the King James Version

1. Christian Booksellers Association, "CBA Bestseller List," *CBA Marketplace,* October 2001.
2. An example is the pamphlet by J. J. Ray, *The Eye Opener* (Junction City, Ore., 1953).
3. D. A. Carson, *The King James Version Debate: A Plea for Realism* (Grand Rapids: Baker, 1979), 34.
4. Ibid., 35.
5. F. F. Bruce, *The Books and the Parchments,* 3d ed. (Old Tappan, N.J.: Revell, 1963), 185.
6. J. Harold Greenlee, *Introduction to New Testament Textual Criticism* (Grand Rapids: Eerdmans, 1964), 61–62.
7. To be more precise, although Westcott and Hort gave the greater

weight to the Alexandrian text over the Byzantine, they gave even greater weight to the manuscripts *Vaticanus* and *Siniaticus,* which they considered to be "neutral texts." Later, sympathetic scholars grouped these two manuscripts with the Alexandrian family. See Carson, *The King James Version Debate,* 41.

8. Edward F. Hills, "The Magnificent Burgon," in *Which Bible?* 5th ed., ed. David Otis Fuller (Grand Rapids: Grand Rapids International Publications, 1975), 101–5.

9. Greenlee, *Introduction to New Testament Textual Criticism,* 133.

10. Ibid., 68.

11. In addition to the Greek manuscripts, also available for study are ancient lectionaries, various translations into other languages, and the writings of the early church fathers. See Greenlee, *Introduction to New Testament Textual Criticism,* 44–58.

12. Ibid., 17.

13. Zane C. Hodges, "The Greek Text of the King James Version," in *Which Bible?* 37.

14. Greenlee, *Introduction to New Testament Textual Criticism,* 81.

15. Carson, *The King James Version Debate,* 47.

16. Eusebius Pamphilus, *Ecclesiastical History* (Grand Rapids: Baker, 1971), 215–16. See also Benjamin G. Wilkinson, "Our Authorized Bible Vindicated," in *Which Bible?* 190–93.

Chapter 11: The Uniqueness of Jesus

1. William Lecky, *History of European Morals from Augustus to Charlemagne* (New York: D. Appleton and Co., 1903), 8.

2. Josh McDowell, *Evidence that Demands a Verdict* (San Bernardino, Calif.: Here's Life Publishers, 1979), 167.

3. Norman L. Geisler and Ronald M. Brooks, *When Skeptics Ask: A Handbook on Christian Evidences* (Wheaton, Ill.: Victor Books, 1990), 116.

4. Tim LaHaye, *Jesus, Who Is He?* (Sisters, Ore.: Multnomah, 1996), 176.

5. Norman Geisler and William Nix, *A General Introduction to the Bible* (Chicago: Moody, 1986), 365–66.

6. Peter Carsten Theide and Matthew D'Ancona, *Eyewitness to Jesus* (New York: Doubleday, 1996), 163.

7. Anonymous, "One Solitary Life," in *Jesus, Who Is He?* by LaHaye, 68.

Chapter 12: The Deity of Christ

1. Millard J. Erickson, *Christian Theology* (Grand Rapids: Baker, 1985), 684–90.

2. Merrill C. Tenney, *The Expositor's Bible Commentary,* vol. 9 (Grand Rapids: Zondervan, 1981), 99.

3. Ibid., 28–29.

4. Henry Bettenson, ed., *Documents of the Christian Church* (New York: Oxford University Press, 1967), 26.

Chapter 13: The Historical Christ: A Response to "From Jesus to Christ"

1. "From Jesus to Christ: The First Christians," PBS broadcast, pts. 1 and 2, 7–8 April 1998 (hereinafter cited in text as FJTC). Transcript obtained from PBS web site: http://www.pbs.org/wgbh/pages/front-line/shows/religion/.

2. John Dominic Crosson, *Jesus: A Revolutionary Biography* (San Francisco: Harper Collins, 1994), 95.

3. Ben Witherington III, *The Jesus Quest: The Third Search for the Jew of Nazareth* (Downers Grove, Ill.: InterVarsity, 1995), 9.

4. C. Stephen Evans, *The Historical Christ and the Jesus of Faith: The Incarnational Narrative as History* (Oxford: Clarendon Press, 1996), 13.

5. Witherington, *The Jesus Quest,* 11.

6. Ibid., 12.

7. Darrel L. Bock, New Testament professor, Dallas Theological Seminary. Telephone conversation with the author, 15 April 1998.

8. Craig L. Blomberg, "Where Do We Start Studying Jesus?" in *Jesus Under Fire,* ed. Michael J. Wilkins and J. P. Moreland (Grand Rapids: Zondervan, 1995), 28.

9. Ibid., 29.

10. Ibid., 28–29.

11. Ibid., 29.

12. Ibid., 30. Material for the remainder of this section was drawn from pages 30–32.

13. See, for example, A. T. Robertson, *A Harmony of the Gospels for Students of the Life of Christ* (New York: Harper & Row, 1950), 201–8.

14. Blomberg, "Where Do We Start Studying Jesus?" 32.

15. Darrell L. Bock, "The Words of Jesus in the Gospels: Live, Jive, or Memorex?" in *Jesus Under Fire,* ed. Michael J. Wilkins and J. P. Moreland (Grand Rapids: Zondervan, 1995), 79.

16. Blomberg, "Where Do We Start Studying Jesus?" 32.

Chapter 14: The Resurrection of Christ

1. Josephus *Antiquities*, trans. by W. Whitson (Peabody, Mass.: Hendrickson, 1987), 18.33.
2. Josh McDowell, *The Resurrection Factor* (San Bernardino, Calif.: Here's Life Publishers, 1981), 66.
3. William McNeil, *A World History* 3d ed. (New York: Oxford University Press, 1979), 163.
4. David Strauss, *The Life of Jesus for the People,* 2d ed. (London: Williams and Norgate, 1879), 1.412.